THE POWER OF LEGACY

*Engaging Generations,
Developing Leadership,
and Planning Succession*

By Charles Leichtweis

© 2023 Charlie Leichtweis, All Rights Reserved. No portion of this book may be reproduced, stored in a retrieval system, or transmitted in any for or by any means—electronic, mechanical, photocopy, recording, scanning, or any other—except for brief quotations in critical reviews or articles, without the prior written permission of the publisher.

Published by EIH Publishing
11432 James Jack Lane
Charlotte, NC 28277

Every effort has been made to obtain permissions for material quoted throughout the book. If any required acknowledgements have been omitted, or any rights overlooked, it is unintentional. Please notify the publisher of any omission, and it will be rectified in future editions.

ISBN 979-8-9890490-4-2
Library of Congress Control Number: 2022912477
Printed in the United States

What Readers Are Saying

Running a family business is challenging enough without having to go it alone. Learning from others' journeys, mistakes, and successes is the best way to evolve one's thinking. Charlie Leichtweis has masterfully compiled stories and insights that, when implemented, will help make your family business legacy a success.

~ *Meghan Juday, Chairman of the Board, IDEAL Industries, Inc.*

The inner workings of a generational family business can be incredibly difficult to navigate, however Charlie has created a roadmap for success. This book is a must-read for every family member involved in their family business, especially those who are looking to pass the business on to the next generation, and those who are yearning to take over from the previous generation. It will help every family avoid the pitfalls of family business ownership and legacy mapping and is something I wish I had when working on succession planning with my father and uncle.

~ *Jamie Shyer, Co-CEO/COO, Zyloware Eyewear*

The Power of Legacy model is a great one to help families to frame their discussions and a way to see the bigger picture, I believe. One sentence that stood out for me was, 'As long as you understand the principles, it's my experience that you can use them to get everyone to agree to move your business into the future, rather than into court.' To agree to move forward is it. It's not about agreeing on *everything* but about agreeing on the *direction*. The Personal Phases section is a really important part of the planning process that gets overlooked too often, and that has consequences.

I really enjoyed it and love the practical approach he takes. The quotes from real family business owners and the questions and reflections at the end of each chapter brought each section to life.

~ Elizabeth Bagger, Founder of Avanti Family Business Advisory, and former Director General of the Institute for Family Business in the UK.

"The Power of Legacy is the definitive guide and an actionable handbook for family businesses at all stages and at any generational inflection point. You'll reap the benefits of Charlie's decades-long experience with family businesses, and the wisdom of countless leaders he has interviewed and supported. As Charlie notes, 'Even families who have figured it out haven't always figured it out. Figuring things out is complicated.' This book will help you through that complication so YOU can be the family member who figures it out!"

~ Katherine J. Armstrong, Founder, The Cusp Connection, LLC

"The Power of Legacy is an excellent guide for family businesses to navigate and embrace numerous challenges to preserve family legacy. I particularly liked how Charlie linked the act of mutual respect with building and sustaining family legacy. In addition, for every challenge to preserve family legacy, Charlie offers helpful tools for family businesses to start conversations and find solutions that benefit both the family and the business."

~ Sandi Thorman, Partner, Greer Walker LLP

"As an HR leader this book spoke to me on multiple levels and provided great insight as well as a clear roadmap to have tough but meaningful conversations. It's a straightforward read for anyone involved in running a family business or coaching someone who does. The first pages start with asking the questions that need to be answered but most are too scared to ask or hear the responses. The following chapters provide a road map to honest and provoking dialogue around legacy, respect, values and the future. It clears the veil of being family in a family business and encourages true business discussions while still respecting one another. The chapter focused on Risk is a great chapter for any business owner or leader – not just a family-owned company.

"I would strongly recommend this book for someone who is working to define the business, the future of the business and how it works with the family's values, phase of life and family identity. You know how to run your business, but this helps you on your journey with your family business."

~ Megan Drulard, CHRO

Table of Contents

WHAT READERS ARE SAYING I
DEDICATION IX
ACKNOWLEDGEMENTS XI
FORWARD 1
INTRODUCTION 3
- *Family Legacy* 4
- *Personal phases* 4
- *Family & Business Architecture* 4
- *Generational Engagement* 5
- *Leadership Development* 5
- *Succession Planning* 5
- *Corporate and Family Governance* 6
- *Risk Management* 6

A NOTE FROM THE AUTHOR 9

CHAPTER 1 – THE ROLE OF RESPECT 13

CHAPTER 2 – EMBRACE CHALLENGES 21
 Governance 31
 Family and Business Architecture including Personal Phases 32
 Succession Planning and Generational Engagement 34
 Risk Management 36
 Overall 37
 Embrace Challenges Thought Starters 38

CHAPTER 3 - LEGACY 41
 Legacy Thought Starters 53

CHAPTER 4 – PERSONAL PHASES 57
1. *Starting a business* 59
2. *Managing a business* 60
3. *Owning the business* 61
4. *Investor* 62
5. *Evolving the business* 63
6. *Pivoting the business* 64
7. *Stepping up or stepping in* 64
8. *Joining the business* 65

Personal Phases Thought Starters *67*
Use the following grid to ask and answer these questions:
.... *67*

CHAPTER 5 – FAMILY AND BUSINESS ARCHITECTURE 69

Family And Business Architecture Thought Starters *77*

CHAPTER 6 – GENERATIONAL ENGAGEMENT 79

Business Skills *86*
Relationship Skills *87*
Communication and respect *87*
Education *87*
Generational Engagement Thought Starters *90*
Example Survey Questionnaire *91*
Industry perspective *92*

CHAPTER 7 – LEADERSHIP DEVELOPMENT 93

Managing Emotions *96*
Communication *97*
The Power of Respect *99*
Being Clear About Results *99*
Leadership Development Thought Starters *101*

CHAPTER 8 – SUCCESSION PLANNING 105

Start Early and Plan Strategically *110*
Identify potential successors! *111*
Develop and train potential successors *113*
Communication *113*
Balance the needs of the business and the family *114*
Financial considerations *115*
Emotional considerations *115*
Succession Planning Thought Starters *117*

CHAPTER 9 – GOVERNANCE 119

Those "ground rules" are governance. *124*
Process *126*
Agreement *126*
Implementation *127*
Governance and Family Values *128*
Governance Thought Starters *129*

CHAPTER 10 – RISK MANAGEMENT 131

Objectives of ERM: *135*

Risk Management Thought Starters 140
CHAPTER 11 – NEXT STEPS 143
One last thought: 145
ABOUT THE AUTHOR 147
A SPECIAL INVITATION 151

Dedication

This book is dedicated to the families who have embraced the challenge of building and managing relationships, both as a family and a business, in order to make the world a better place now and for generations to come.

Acknowledgements

To those who contributed to the wisdom in this book:

I would like to express my thanks of gratitude to clients and leaders who shared their insights, wisdom, quotes, and thoughts with me. I'm always impressed with the organizations and leaders who continually strive to be better for the benefit of others. I'm fortunate to work with the leaders who participated in this book, and many more throughout my career. I hope that their wisdom supports your growth.

Walter Davis, Founding Member, Peachtree Providence Partners

Ashley D. Joyce, Chairman, The Duchossois Family Foundation

William Goodspeed, Board Chair & Independent Director

Tina Greenbaum, CEO, Mastery Under Pressure

Tom Goldblatt, Managing Partner, Ravinia Capital

Meghan Juday, Chairman of the Board, IDEAL Industries

David Judson, Founder & CEO, JRR Solutions

Steve Kosmalski, Fortune 100 Consumer Products Turnaround Executive

Bill McLean, Partner, Richter

Jim Phillip, CEO, Phillip's Flowers & Gifts

Torsten Pieper, Associate Professor, University of North Carolina, Charlotte

Kim Adele-Randall, CEO, Authentic Achievements

Jamie Shyer, Co-CEO/COO, Zyloware Eyewear

Trey Taylor, Managing Director, Taylor Family Office

Tony Tennaro, Principal Chair, C12 Charlotte

Phil Wellington, VP, GM, Siemens Healthineers

Sherry Winn, Two-Time Olympian, CEO, The Winning Leadership Company, Author of *Winning Leadership: Seven Secrets to Being a Truly Powerful Leader*

Paul S. Gumbinner, President (ret) The Gumbinner Company

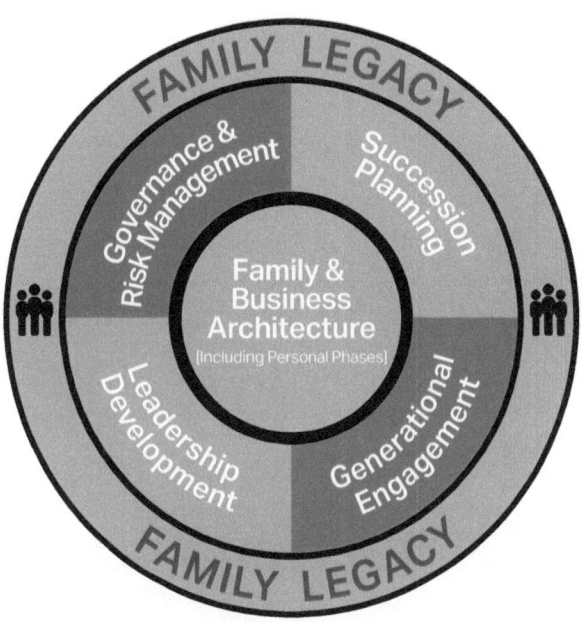

FORWARD

Family Legacy is a powerful creation by a family based on who and how they show up in the world. It is a unifying force, shared and passed on, molded, and changed over time by each generation, and lived every day and kept alive by the family members. It matters to all forms of family business, and it takes time and commitment to work out what you want your collective legacy to be and how you wish to create it.

That's why I was extremely excited to read Charles Leichtweis' book, *The Power of Legacy*.

This book is the perfect blend of helpful truths, excellent suggestions of 'how to,' as well as powerful family business examples. There are very incisive and helpful questions at the end of each chapter that will help you to assess and address every aspect of your family firm to make better and more informed decisions as you move forward.

It invites you to look at every part of your family business and their interconnectedness from legacy creation to business and family architecture, to generational engagement, leadership development, succession planning, family and business governance, and risk management. It also invites you to look at these aspects through the lens of what Charlie refers to as "Personal Phases" because it matters whether you are starting, running, owning, or investing in a company. Each stage requires a different type of relationship with the family and the business.

No matter where you are on your family business journey, this book is a powerful companion, and it invites you to reflect on every part of your family and your business.

This is a book to engage with and work with, not just to read and put on a shelf, but one to talk to family members about and keep coming back to. Doing so will have the power to transform your family business and to assure you can co-create your legacy, so your family can continue the journey together across generations.

I know Charlie's book will be an immensely helpful resource to your family on your legacy journey.

~ Elizabeth Bagger, Founder of Avanti Family Business Advisory, and former Director General of the Institute for Family Business in the UK.

Introduction

Building a business is hard. Building a family business is harder. But the hardest thing is trying to build your family business into **a legacy that endures** for generations to come.

You're not alone, and a lot of great minds have done a lot of great thinking on these issues. The desire to create a legacy is almost universal, and the challenge of doing that through family succession has been the theme of every great drama, from Sophocles' *Oedipus Rex* to Shakespeare's *Richard III*, to Arthur Miller's *All My Sons*.

Every business wants to grow and profit, but family-run businesses have an added component—they want to sustain and nurture as well. And sometimes those needs are not in sync.

How a family negotiates their company governance and management can either build a lasting legacy (Walmart, BMW, Berkshire Hathaway, Ford, Rockefeller), or end in a bankruptcy sale six months after the founder dies. Between those two extremes are thousands of companies that struggle with the added dynamics of family relationships and family governance.

Tolstoy wrote, "Happy families are all alike; every unhappy family is unhappy in its own way."

You may have picked up this book because you're struggling with your own family business dynamics. Often, in the day-to-day effort of running your business and managing your family, it can be difficult to separate the different elements that interact. This book will help you break it down into discrete, manageable parts.

Through my workshops, talks, writing, and interventions, I've helped hundreds of family-run businesses find their unique way to solve their governance and relationship issues. For some, the results have been stability and success, which can endure for generations. For others, it's meant stability and success that made the business an attractive investment or purchase opportunity. Or sometimes it meant the current owners could pivot and move the business in directions never before imagined.

There are issues *every* business face: Risk Management, Growth, Strategic Planning, Investing, and more. **Family-run businesses must address six additional overlapping challenges that need to be considered.**

- **Family** *Legacy*

Surrounding and defining all family-owned, family-run businesses is the underlying question, "Why?" Why are you doing this? Who are you doing this for? How does your business support your family values? Has anyone in your family ever articulated those values? Does every family member share a common vision of the future?

- **Personal phases**

Understanding where family members are in their journey allows founders and subsequent generations to navigate through transitions, ensure long-term success of the family business and achieve the desired family legacy. Are members starting, running, owning, or investing in a company Are family members moving in the right direction? Do family members need help getting to next phase?

- **Family & Business Architecture**

The structure of the business, and how that connects to the structure of the family, lies at the core of all of these challenges, and drives all business decisions. What does it mean when successful family business owners say, "What's best for the business must come first when making decisions?" Do the business owners understand the balance between recruiting the best person for the job or the best-available relative? Are participants of the same generation at different stages of professional development? What happens if you bypass a family member in favor of a more qualified outsider? How does that choice impact both the family and the business? Do family members have a voice?

- **Generational Engagement**

    Providing a voice for all family members and valuing everyone's opinions and contributions through a culture of collaboration, open communication and mutual respect will ensure that the business remains successful for many years to come. What phase of life is each family member in? Have senior family members considered when they'll move from founder to manager, manager to owner, owner to investor, or step aside completely? Are the younger generations ready to take over, or move on? Has each successive generation been surveyed and involved in the future of the business? How soon should future generations be engaged?

- **Leadership Development**

    One of the biggest challenges that family businesses face is developing leadership experience and creating meaningful opportunities for family members. How are family members evaluated and developed as leaders? How are new family participants brought on board? Is there a useful, realistic process for bringing on new officers, or is it just "plug and play"? Is there a method for developing future family board members?

- **Succession Planning**

    A critical component of building a family legacy is to identify potential successors and create a plan for the transition of leadership. Who's going to run which part of the business, and when? Who are the family members who won't even discuss this issue? Which family members are truly qualified to be senior managers, advisors, directors, or owners? How do you maintain family harmony and diversity principles when selecting family leaders? How do you select non-family members for leadership roles in the business? What should a family employment policy look like?

- **Corporate and Family Governance**

    Are your business rules written in a form everyone can understand and observe? What about family governance rules? Understanding what governance is, and how *family governance* and *corporate governance* fit together is crucial. Are there outside advisors, or a board of directors who can provide an independent point of view? Are key owners even comfortable with the word "outside?" How will the family provide oversight without losing control? What decision-making rules can the family abide by?

- **Risk Management**

    To create value, family businesses must manage and take appropriate risks. Identification of potential risk is a key element of strategic planning. It can also help you identify opportunities. Have you assessed the risks in your organization? What risks are you willing to take to remain innovative, achieve your business goals and build value?

Each of these challenges has a different answer for every business. But you must continually address each of them if your family business is to succeed and grow. I hope you'll start to see how each of these areas impacts your family, and business, and how you can approach them.

I've written this book to help all family businesses of every size understand their minefields and map a way forward. You will find in-depth, real-life examples of each area, and helpful tips and exercises you can use to bring your entire family into alignment. Just as important, I've included a self-

Introduction

help "Thought Starters" section at the end of each chapter. You can use them to get the conversation going in your company and in your family, or as a road map to planning the future.

You'll find dozens of anecdotes, shared experiences, and family stories in this book; however, you may not find a situation that exactly matches yours. That's okay. As long as you understand the principles, you can use them to get everyone to agree to move your business into the future, rather than into court.

The oldest continuously operating business in the world is family-owned and family-run. *Nishiyama Onsen Keiunkan* is a hot springs hotel located in Japan, and has been in continuous operation a little more than 1300 years, since 705 A.D. It's been managed, nurtured, grown, and sustained by the Mahito family for 52 generations.

Will your family still be running your business successfully 52 generations from now, or ten, or even three? It will depend entirely on the choices you make in *your* generation. The Mahito family proves it can be done.

A Note from the Author

Have you heard any of these statements on your journey?

"I'm 33 years old, yet my grandfather still sees me as the ten-year-old that sat at his feet at Christmas."

"I can't work with my cousin. He won't listen, and I can never get my point across."

"My father isn't ready to let go of control of the business. What should I do?"

"No one should get a position of leadership in this business before me."

"We can grow significantly in next five years, but I'm not sure how to get my family to work together."

"My brother constantly criticizes my work. I have no confidence in my decision making."

"Stop the screaming."

There are a number of distinct realities that create challenges for all family-owned businesses that you don't have in other organizations. For example, you can't change the history of your family relationships. You can't "fire" a family member from the family. You can't walk away from hurt feelings after a contentious interaction, or pretend it didn't happen, and you can't create a successful legacy without respectful engagement with each other.

You'll see examples in some of these realities in the words of the business owners quoted in this book who have managed to address them.

We know that it takes time and effort to address these challenges. As I've helped family organizations over the years, I've learned that these realities are not static. They don't just occur once and are then fixed forever. They can, and sometimes do, reoccur as the family and the business evolve through cycles and generations. I've found that best way to address the challenges is through an understanding of the elements of creating a successful legacy, how they affect relationships, and how they are connected. It's within this framework that the variability of the emotional and business cycles can be managed successfully over time.

The elements of a successful family business need to be broken down into distinct steps that allow you to manage your legacy *and* your business down a path to repetitive success. That's what this book is all about.

I've worked in or for family businesses for nearly 40 years. I've been a non-family member of the senior leadership team, a founder of a consulting practice that specializes in family business dynamics, and served as a member of the Board of Directors for family businesses, large and small.

My mission is to help families and family-owned businesses understand and manage the elements of legacy, to provide the best path for your family and your business, and to create a sustainable, successful legacy for the benefit of future generations.

Chapter 1

The Role of Respect

There is no legacy without mutual respect.

Everything you will read in this book,

...every lesson

...every tip

...every suggestion

...every idea

.... every possible path forward will only succeed if there is true, honest respect among all the management, owners, and family members. Respect is near and dear to my heart. It helped heal wounds of communication in my family and it powers my work and relationships. In my book on leadership, The Power of *Respect in Business*, I discuss many examples of how respect powers good leadership. On "The Power of Respect" podcast, I interview leaders of family-owned, family-run businesses and I close each episode with the statement "Respect builds trust, trust builds relationship, and relationships are the key to Leadership."

Professor Torsten Pieper, a globally recognized expert in family business, believes staying together as a family is paramount to facing the ups and downs of business. In my discussions with him he pointed out the need to keep coming back to the focus of moving forward together despite the challenges:

> "You have to be able to feel as a group, and that means as an ownership group, as a family group, that...we can recover from failure, that we can get through this if we all stick together. And if we don't stick together, then we realize we're not going to make it. That's why this notion of togetherness and cohesion is so important, especially in families, because we are much, much stronger if we are in a group than if we go our separate ways. That requires respect, because it might be that we have some people in the group who are just not compatible with one another from the outset, even though they're still members of the family and we somehow need to make it work. I have to overcome

my ego, give others the benefit of the doubt, and do certain things that need to happen for the benefit of everybody else."
~ *Torstein Pieper, Associate Professor, University of North Carolina, Charlotte*

I've found **respect is the most effective way to accomplish decision-making and achieve harmony,** at least to the extent that you can. "Respect" means just what it says that we take the time to actually hear and try to understand what people are saying and where they're coming from. It involves listening longer to people whether we agree with them or not. Respect does not mean unanimous agreement. As the 18th Century French author and philosopher, Voltaire, was purported to have said, "I disapprove of what you say, but I will defend to the death your right to say it."

If we strive to listen longer, we often find that where they were actually going with the discussion may be different than what we assumed while we were too anxious to talk over them.

"Ninety-ten-ninety rule: 90% of the time you should be listening. And the 10% of the time you're talking, 90% of that should be questions." ~ *Tom Goldblatt, Managing Partner, Ravinia Capital*

Another concept that I link to the concept of "listen longer" is, "If you are right now, you will be right later." So you can afford to listen without interrupting to make your point. This demonstrates respect for the people you are speaking with, and they will recognize that they are being heard.

Respect does not mean consensus is required. For example, I have a client whose family business is run by four family members, three brothers and an uncle (they were also the shareholders). One of the three brothers is the appointed CEO. As I was taking time to understand their business and their vision, I noticed that there was an unwritten theme. In the interest of family harmony, all decisions required *consensus* among the four family members.

I pointed out to them that all four of them knew the business very well, were very intelligent, had strong courage of conviction, and had great perspectives to consider when making decisions. I also pointed out that a group with those dynamics makes it almost impossible to reach consensus. However, decisions had to be made to move the business forward, and leadership had the responsibility to choose from the alternatives for the decision to be followed.

The family does not have to agree; it's not a matter of consensus. While you want to gather everybody's ideas, have them understand the context, and let them have their say, at some point the information needs to inform a decision. It's a combination of hearing everything, and then being able to turn that into action. Bill McLean is someone who I have had the pleasure of collaborating with on processes related to generational engagement. He's a partner in a Canadian consulting firm, Richter, focused on the intersection of business and family, much like my firm, Experts In How. As a guest on my podcast, describing how respect informs decision making, he put it this way:

> "Voice does not have to equal vote, but voice is respected. Voice creates an environment for ideation and sharing thoughts, and all those things that can inform the vote without dragging things on to the point where it grinds down to a halt. You cannot achieve a decision when you're trying for absolute consensus across the board." ~ *Bill McLean, Partner, Richter*

Finally, if you truly respect each other's opinions and points of view, it makes it easier to set it all aside (business) and continue to care for each other (family). Or, as Jamie Shyer pointed out, everything starts when you come to work and ends when you go home at night.

"We quickly learned how to separate business from family. My dad taught me that we could argue during the day about business, but at the end of the day, you sit down, you have dinner together, and you enjoy your time together. We see a lot of family businesses not make it because they don't know how to do that." ~*Jamie Shyer, Co-CEO/COO, Zyloware Eyewear*

The result for his family business of this approach to communication and respect has been to celebrate their 100-year anniversary in 2023.

As you read this book, and as you plan on ways to build and sustain your legacy, always keep this idea of respect in the front of your mind. Others will respect you and you will respect yourself a lot more if you do.

Chapter 2

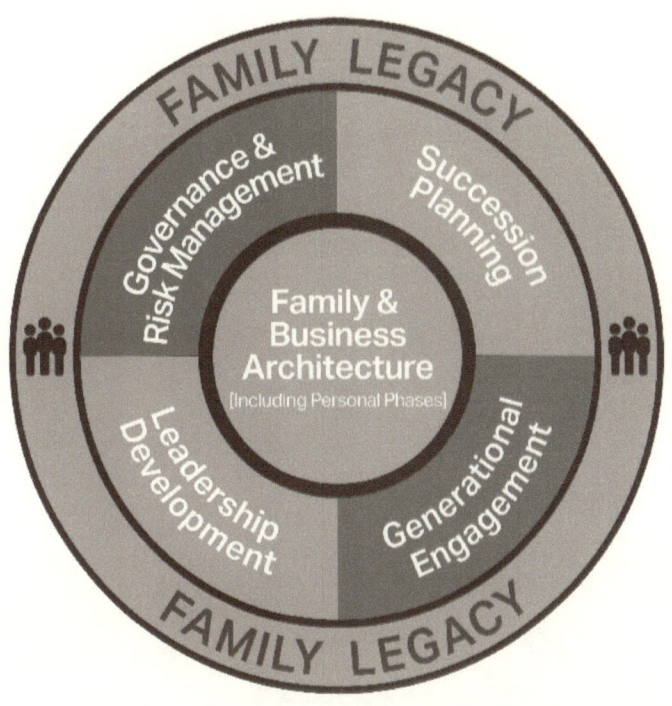

Embrace Challenges

I mentioned earlier that the elements of a successful family business need to be broken down into distinct steps that allow you to manage your legacy *and* your business down a path to repetitive success. That's what this book is all about.

At the most basic level, the elements of legacy for all family-owned, family-run businesses look like this:

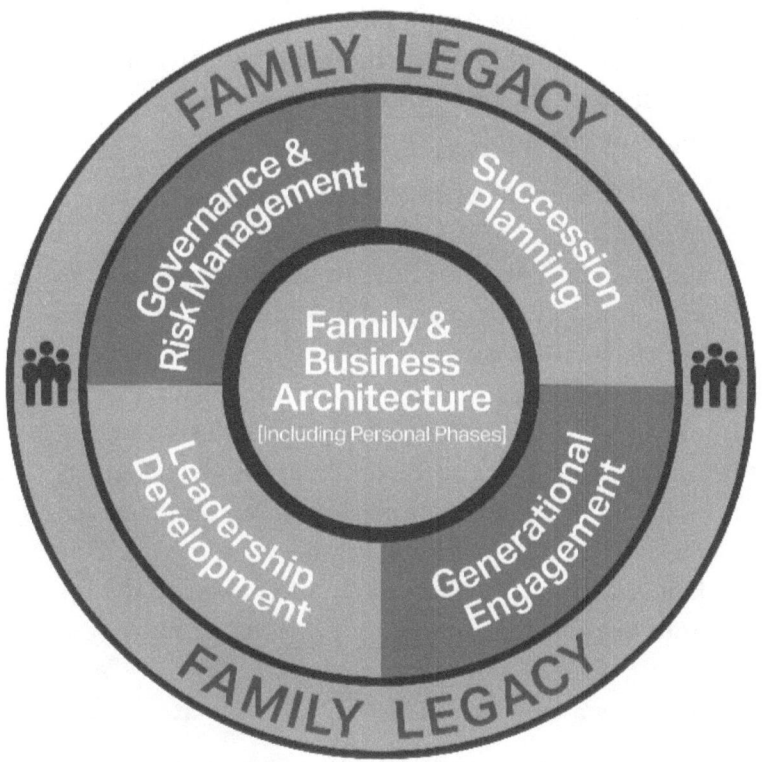

Many family businesses get into trouble when the relationships between these elements are poorly understood, or not connected through education, engagement, shared experiences, and constant communication across the multiple generations and branches of the family. In order to ensure your legacy, you must consider, understand, and address each of these interdependent elements.

That model is a map to this entire book, and to your future success. In this overview you will learn what each element is, and in the following chapters, you will come to understand how each of them works, what to consider about each element, and how they're interrelated.

Study that diagram for a moment. Every successful family business is held together by that outer circle, "Family Legacy." **That legacy is what you choose it to be. Torsten Pieper is a friend and colleague with international expertise in family business. He shared his thoughts on the challenge of family legacy in this quote and shares his wisdom throughout this book.**

> "We see families manage their businesses in an extremely professional, ethical, sustainable way because they see this is part of their responsibility. But at the end of the day, for many families the business is just a vehicle, a means to accomplish an important mission, a higher purpose. And if you take that orientation, apply it to the Rockefellers, it makes perfect sense to say, 'Look, as long as you achieve whatever you want to achieve as a family, if it's not oil and gas and railroads, then pick something else, especially if it suits your goals better, aligns with your values, and gives you the opportunity to have more fun together as a family, by all means, do.'" ~ *Torsten Pieper, Associate Professor, University of North Carolina, Charlotte*

Phillip's Flowers and Gifts is an award-winning family business which will be celebrating 100 years of operation in 2023. They are a client of mine and Jim Phillip; CEO shared his perspective on the importance of family values with respect to legacy. More about their story and success later in this book.

> "I think another common factor that you find in multi-generation family businesses like ours, is that there's a set of core values that are important to keep the family together to solidify the priorities of life." ~ *Jim Phillip, CEO, Phillip's Flowers & Gifts*

Embrace Challenges

Before we go on, ask yourself what words you would write as your desired (or current) family legacy in that outer ring. Legacy is often defined as "something that is passed on," but it can take many forms. A legacy may be of one's faith, ethics, and core values. A legacy may be money or assets. It may come from character or reputation.

A legacy may change over generations. Today the Rockefeller Foundation is a very different legacy than John D. Rockefeller's Standard Oil Company. The intentional decision to pursue a legacy can provide guidance and inspiration. To achieve your legacy, you need to address each element of the circle.

Trey Taylor is CEO of his family-owned, family-run business, Taylor Family Office, as well as an author and family business advisor. He joined me as a guest on my podcast, "The Power of Respect," to describe the significant challenges he faced after a series of sudden deaths in the family which led to the need for him to unexpectedly take over the family business. The suddenness of the changes in the family led required managing and sustaining a legacy with little or no time to prepare.

In addition to running Taylor Insurance Services, he helped migrate the family's legacy from the core insurance business to a philanthropic organization, Taylor Family Office, that supports other family-owned, family-run businesses. To achieve that success, Trey had to address all six challenges listed in the introduction.

Consider this excerpt from an interview with him on "The Power of Respect" podcast:

"We have three generations in our primary business... I took it over from my brother before he passed in 2019. When I was younger, my dad said to me, "Don't come into this business. Go do something else." He felt that the business was a little constrictive and we had enough family members in the business.

"Then dad passed away unexpectedly, and our succession plan didn't hold up. I ended up coming back and eventually becoming the CEO all within the space of 30 days—a business that I was never supposed to be in, didn't have any affinity to, and didn't really have any knowledge about. My training in the business was virtually non-existent except for what I had observed secondhand for 30-something years, just watching the family run the business." ~ *Trey Taylor, CEO, Taylor Insurance Services, Managing Director, Taylor Family Office*

In fewer than 150 words he cited all six challenges he and his family faced.

"We have three generations in our primary business... I took it over from my brother before he passed in 2019. When I was younger, my dad said to me, "Don't come into this business. Go do something else." He felt that the business was a little constrictive **[1: Family Legacy]** and we had enough family members in the business.

Then dad passed away unexpectedly, and our succession plan didn't hold up. **[5: Succession Planning]** I ended up coming back and eventually becoming the CEO all within the space of 30 days **[6: Corporate Governance]**—a business that I was never supposed to be in, **[2: Business & Family Architecture]** didn't have any affinity to, didn't really have any knowledge about. My training in the business was virtually non-existent **[4: Leadership Development]** except for what I had observed secondhand for 30 something years, **[3: Generational Engagement]** just watching the family run the business."

Talk to anyone who runs a family-owned business and they'll tell you the same thing. They're still trying to figure it out. As you can see from Trey, even families who *have* figured

Embrace Challenges

it out haven't *always* figured it out. Figuring things out is complicated. The journey is not a straight line. Many factors come into play and the solution can change over time as family structure, individual personalities, economic conditions, regulatory requirements, and more, change. Fear of the unknown is natural. When deciding what needs to change for your family or your business can be scary, because the future result of that change is unknown. It can feel more comfortable not to change because we are familiar with how things are done today. The problem with not recognizing the need for change is that you will fail to achieve our goals as a family or a business.

> "Things change around us. [We hear owners say] 'We know the plan is not working, but still, we're unwilling to change course because so much effort was poured into this. We saw that very clearly through the pandemic. [Some] businesses were able to change and pivot in a brilliant and very fast way. And others were not, because they just could not grasp that the world around them had changed and that the old ways of operating suddenly no longer worked." ~ *Torsten Pieper, Associate Professor, University of North Carolina, Charlotte*

Do you feel the pressure of figuring out what your legacy is, and how to go about it? Do you feel the pressure to creating and abide by one singular plan to achieve success? These are some of the statements we hear from clients that add pressure to the issue of creating a legacy:

"Our family business legacy is in our hands."

"Creating a successful legacy is our hardest business problem."

"The problem with creating a sustainable legacy with our family business is our *family*."

"The business you're building *is* your legacy."

I've helped families begin to frame their legacy, or focus an existing legacy, by starting with describing your family values.

Your family's legacy—the way(s) in which your business expresses your shared family values—is the all-defining architecture. Like a blueprint for a building, it frames and informs all decisions. Meghan Juday is the chair of a large 107-year-old family business that was founded by her great grandfather. She has grown up hearing about and seeing the challenges of her family's business. She describes the importance of values within the architecture that shapes a legacy:

> "Our family values are Inclusiveness, Transparency, Relationships, Engagement, Empowerment and Stewardship. The thing that's interesting, when you have family values, you don't do just one. Every decision must fit *all* those values. it's like a constant litmus test that you can use in developing policies and making decisions." ~ *Meghan Juday, Chair of the Board, IDEAL Industries*

At the heart of the diagram depicting the elements of legacy is Family and Business Architecture, the operational expression of your business and your legacy. While "Family Architecture" and "Business Architecture" are different, they constantly *compete* for importance in all decisions your organization will make.

When we add the overlapping issues of Governance, Generational Engagement, Leadership Development and Succession Planning, the boundaries between them aren't so neat. Plus—and this will be a recurring theme in this book—you must manage two parallel organizations: the family and the business. Both organizations have the usual individual issues (jockeying for position, egos, private agendas, and more). The challenge for the operational team and the ownership team of the family is to remember which "organization" takes precedence. Even though I've shown the diagram as separate issues, they almost always overlap like this:

Within all the potentially complex interrelationships of influence and decision making, there can be a tendency for each constituent to want to go in their own direction. **I've seen**

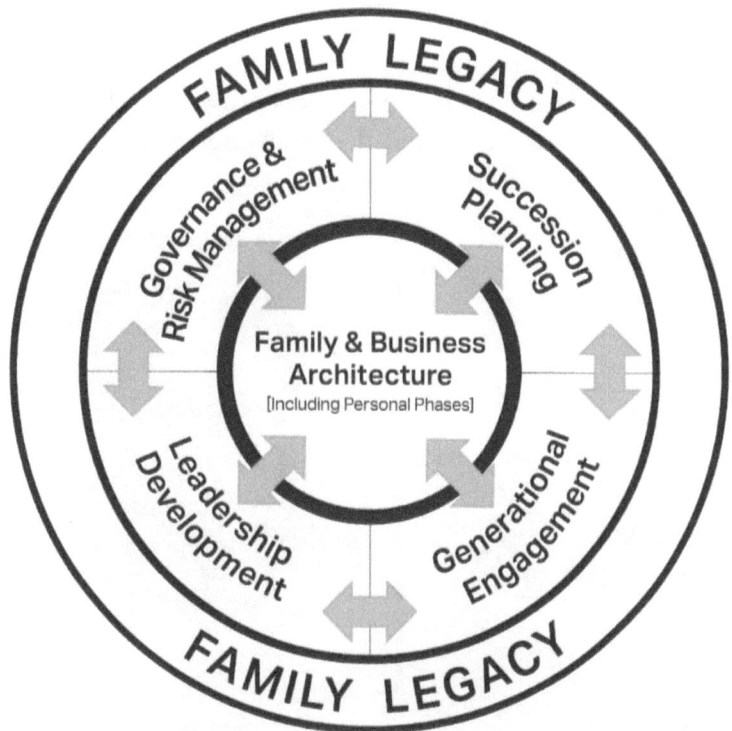

client companies get out of balance when they don't realize the connection between the family and the business. The business is the engine that provides for the family. When family members put their own needs before the needs of the business, the business can become drained of the resources (strategic options, cash, talent) that allow it to continue to provide for the legacy of the family. Trey Taylor describes the priorities between family and business.

> "Generational engagement, succession planning, and a governance structure that allows for voices to be heard can lead to making decisions that appropriately address

the needs of the business so it can support the long-term needs of the family. When it comes down to a choice that benefits the family versus a choice that benefits the business, family owners and experts agree that the business comes first."
~ *Trey Taylor, Managing Director, Taylor Family Office*

To choose the right path, you must understand your own family dynamics and your own business prospects. The reason can be seen when we expand the small circle labeled Family and Business Architecture at the core:

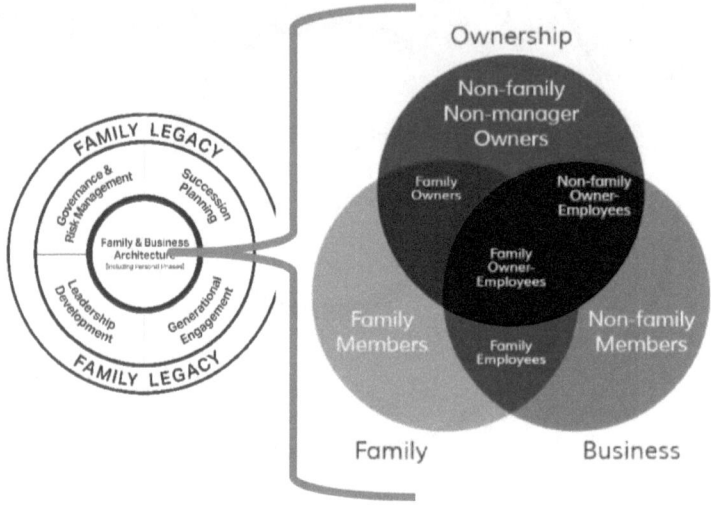

This Three-Circle Model of the Family Business System was developed by Renato Tagiuri and John Davis at Harvard Business School and was circulated in working papers starting in 1978. It was first published in Davis's doctoral dissertation, *The Influence of Life Stages on Father-Son Work Relationships in Family Companies*, in 1982. In 1996, the Family Business Review published it in Tagiuri and Davis's classic article, "Bivalent Attributes of the Family Firm."

The diagram represents three interdependent and overlapping systems in a family enterprise: family, ownership, and business. For a family business to function effectively, each system must understand how to interact with and support the other two systems. In addition, people within each system should appreciate which decisions are theirs to make.

Governance

"Governance" is a hot-button term for family-owned, family-run businesses. Family members often bristle or, worse, shut down when they hear the word. They think it means someone's going to be brought in from outside the family, or worse, from inside the family but outside the business, to tell them how to do things.

There are cases where I've asked owners about their governance structure, and they give me ac concerned look and state that they don't need someone telling them what to do. I then ask, "What do you do when you want to make business decisions about where to spend money?" They almost always describe the data they gather and the analysis they perform and the approval process they require for spending certain large amounts. At that point I know they understand governance because the process they describe is the decision-making process that *is* governance. At that point I'm able to help them review and improve their governance policies and procedures where necessary.

When you think about the elements of governance and decision making, I'm talking about having a defined process and the information you need to make an informed decision, without having to explain it to 20 (or more) owners.

You also start seeing governance as a resource or tool. There are other people involved whom you can turn to for input and advice, and the interaction of all parties in the family *and* in the business is critical. This interaction, support, and decision making *is* governance. Family governance is the process of facilitating communication, support and decision making between family members, as well as between the family and the business. It also provides a forum for education, constructive discussion, problem solving, and decisions about the family as it relates to the business, as well as how the business relates to the family. But without an overarching, formal structure, there's no way to move the business forward.

Family and Business Architecture including Personal Phases

Each of those overlapping circles helps determine where the business is going and whether it'll get there or not. The important thing to keep in mind is that it's not a linear journey. It's circular and evolves over time. I think of it as an ever-enlarging circle, like a nautilus, with each successive—and successful—generation having to manage a larger and larger company, and a more and more complex family ownership structure. The architecture will need to adapt over the evolution of personal phases and evolution of the business itself.

When you start with the founding generation, you'll get a very different read on each of those components than in successive generations. In fact, some of those components may not have occurred to them at that time. If you think about Governance and Risk Management as the process of decision making, often the founding entrepreneurs are going to say *all* the decisions are theirs to make. They understand why they started the business. They believe they understand the business. They understand how much money they have, or need, to grow it. And they believe they know how the business can best grow within the timeframe. But what happened in 1923, or 1963, or 2003, is very different than what's happening today. The challenge, indeed, the struggle, is to bridge the communication connection between the circles that influence decision making and the stages of each generation involved. Zyloware Eyewear experienced a conflict that I've seen many times.

> "In the early 1960's when my father and uncle decided to outsource eyeglasses for the first time, they went to France to work with a small factory called Bollé, which we all know now for ski goggles.

> "My grandfather was livid! He said, 'You do not go somewhere else and make eyeglasses. *We* make the glasses. That's what we *do*. We don't go somewhere else!' He then said, 'I'm not dealing with you two kids. You don't know what you're doing,' and he left, went home, and stayed home. A few months later when he started seeing the sales reports that his sons would send them home to him, of how great things were with this new eyeglass frame, respect was earned, and he came back." ~ *Jamie Shyer, Co-CEO/COO, Zyloware Eyewear*

The result of the conflict described by Jamie Shyer was a product development pivot that allowed for significant growth for the company. Evolutionary changes make a difference in how the business is run and how the family members relate and interact with it.

The Zyloware example above as well as the Phillip's flowers example below, represent the impact of a certain generation being comfortable with the way they see the family and business structure based on their phase in life. The fear of change can cripple the path for growth in any organization. We've been successful helping businesses recognize the family governance role and the business governance role within the structure and develop communication strategies and processes that allow management to run the business effectively, while providing appropriate authority and control for the family.

> "When a business starts at the founder's level, it's dominated by one person's vision, one person's decisions. It's very autocratic, and I'm sure my grandfather was that way. When my father finished his military service and completed his degree in business at Northwestern University, he came into the business. A new shopping center was being built west of Cicero. He got excited about that, but his father thought that was the dumbest thing in the world. Why would you separate your resources, divide them, take on more overhead, more

rent, more utilities?" ~ *Jim Phillip, CEO, Phillip's Flowers & Gifts*

The interaction of all the elements that go into governance, whether it's family governance or corporate governance, change over time depending on the number of people involved, the complexities of the market environments, and when they're doing it.

> "As the years go by and the generations become involved in the business, of course you're going to get a more complex setup. You have multiple family members that are coming in, and there can be some struggles with that whole approach to centralized decision making." ~ *Bill McLean, Partner, Richter*

The complexity grows generation-by-generation. One of my clients is currently transitioning to G4. They have more than twice the number of family members in G4 than in G3. Some are actively involved, while some have moved into different careers and live far afield. The solution is to appropriately engage *all* those people in the family governance side, and how it's operated. **Corporate governance doesn't need to evolve as constantly or as often, but family governance must evolve along with the size of the family, and the breadth of where they're living.** We'll look at those distinctions in each section of the book.

Succession Planning and Generational Engagement

Succession planning and generational engagement are inextricably related. What comes first, though, is generational *engagement*. That's a key to being able to do succession planning in a way that appropriately serves the business *and* the family. It begins with respect and its impact on relationships as a necessary component to help manage change and move forward in a positive way.

Embrace Challenges

The business needs to be *directed* by management and *guided* by the family. In some cases, there's an outside advisory board, sometimes a board of directors, or sometimes a team of trusted family advisors. That's the constituency who determines how the business should be run. Succession planning involves determining whether anyone has the skills required to properly direct the business.

Continued success requires leaders to have a technical skill set for managing and guiding a particular business. For example, if it's a manufacturing business, how do you run manufacturing? What do you know about the supply chain? What do you know about global markets? What do you know about this business's markets or distribution channels or customer bases? The skill set can be any of those. Nobody knows all of that, but the business governance side needs to make sure those skills are present in the leadership team.

If a family has someone with technical ability *and* governance skills, that's a home run. Unfortunately, that's rare. As family members begin to grow up and work through their education and career paths, they don't necessarily fine-tune their training to focus on the needs of the family business. There are, however, other skill sets that come into play that an outside person does not immediately bring to the table. To participate in the decision-making process, it is important to recognize that a family member also needs to have skills in areas such as understanding the family values, having the trust of the greater family, being able to disagree with family members yet get along with them, and being able to speak up to voice their opinion when necessary. Family involvement is critical to the future of every family business. I've seen this throughout my career. Torsten Pieper describes it through his research.

> "Families give organizations an element of longevity that's just unmatched by other organizations. When you see some of these really old family businesses—I studied some of them as part of my dissertation back in Germany, companies that are 350 or so years old—

often these companies go through remarkable changes. Many resemble nothing of what they started out as. Keeping the family involved and engaged allows companies to be able to continue through change and serve their customers, markets, suppliers, and various other stakeholders." ~ *Torsten Pieper, Associate Professor, University of North Carolina, Charlotte*

That's why generational engagement is so important. Generational engagement goes back to understanding who the people are in the family, how they relate to one another, and other key elements. Do they have the respect of the family? Are they willing to have a significant argument or disagreement with the family and then bring it to resolution? Do they understand the family values? Those things are very important. Even If they don't have the technical skills, the family negotiation skills are definitely what you want on the board or in management. You must keep in mind how **generational engagement will determine whether the family members are more-ready or less-ready for succession planning.**

The key is running the business in a way that serves both the family interests as well as the business. That's part of the natural cycle of family businesses.

Risk Management

Risk Management is a mix of family tolerance and business necessity. It's a very specific, best-in-class ability to do what I call the two A's of risk management, *anticipation* and *action*. Most of the time we want to be aware of an issue in advance (anticipation), and then be able to react (action). An example of how we help clients with this is in the case of economic uncertainty. By identifying the economic indices that affect the supply chain and markets of our clients, we are able to create a "Cockpit Chart" of key leading indicators to monitor circumstances that require decisions by the company. We've helped clients minimize working capital investment, create pricing strategies, and maintain the highest levels of customer service. Other times, we must address an issue we're not prepared for (action). No one was prepared for how to do business when Covid arrived in 2020. To anticipate or take action, you must know the components that can affect your business in a potential risk situation. You need a best-in-class model to turn to.

It's a framework. Every detail doesn't apply to everyone, but if you think about it in terms of the framework (which I will explain in Chapter 9) you will see the page headings, rows, and column headings that give you an idea of how to begin to look at it in your business. What's going on? What risks do you see? Which components are critical? Is it trending up or down? When you look at risk management, you start to see it as a key part of governance because governance is about decision making. If you make decisions only when the problem clobbers you in the head, you're not doing your job. Keep in mind that managing risk is also managing opportunity.

Overall

Three elements go into giving your business clarity and control over all challenges:

- **Shared Vision:** All business participants—owners, family, and employees—understand where the business is going.
- **Shared Priorities:** All family members—owners, employees, and non-owners—understand the goals of the family legacy.
- **Mutual Respect:** Even if there are disagreements, there's respect for one another, personally, and professionally.

As you look at the different components of your business, and as you read the chapters of this book, make note of the places you believe either your business *or* your family is stuck. As you start to untangle the different challenges, you will start to see what needs to be addressed and the path forward.

Embrace Challenges Thought Starters

Download the 8½ x 11 printable forms from: ExpertsInHow.com/thought-starters

Can you separate, even a little, the six challenges your business faces?

1. Family Legacy
2. Family and Business Architecture including personal phases
3. Generational Engagement
4. Leadership Development
5. Succession Planning
6. Risk management

If you're able to see those separate issues, which one is the #1 challenge your family business faces?

Rank them from 1, "most important" to 6, "must be dealt with sooner rather than later."

_____ Family Legacy

_____ Family and Business Architecture including Personal Phases

_____ Generational Engagement

_____ Leadership Development

_____ Succession Planning

_____ Risk Management

Embrace Challenges 39

Do your owners and managers agree on the three key elements of business clarity and control?

	Full	Part	None
Shared Vision	☐	☐	☐
Shared Priorities	☐	☐	☐
Mutual Respect	☐	☐	☐

What steps must you take to bring your family and business into agreement?

_____

_____

_____

_____

_____

_____

_____

_____

_____

_____

_____

_____

Chapter 3

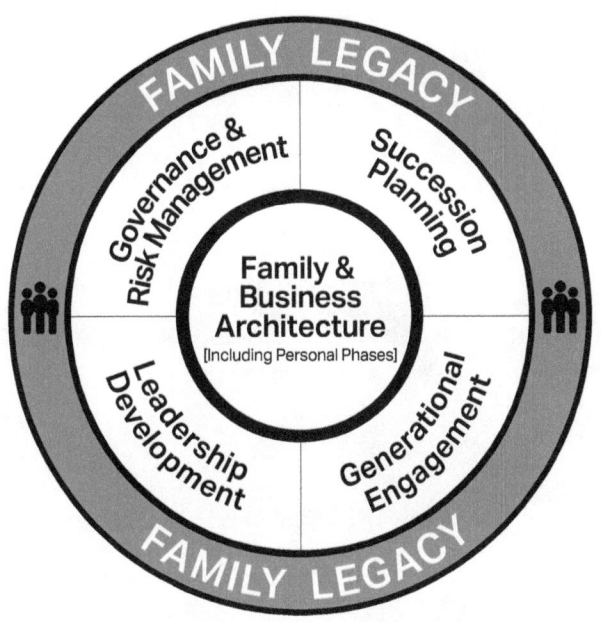

Legacy

"Service to others is the rent you pay for your room here on earth." ~ Muhammad Ali

What's your legacy going to be, and who will it affect? Will it be your estate? Your heirs? Your reputation? Your business? Your employees? Your customers? Your friends and neighbors? Are you thinking multiple generations down the road? What about your immediate family? Your parents and children? Aunts and uncles? Nephews and nieces? What about your larger "family," your employees, your neighbors, your friends? What about your legacy for customers, the communities you do business in, and generations to come?

Legacy is a term that can be difficult to define in ways that you can apply to the specific situation in which you find yourself. It can seem incredibly complicated when psychologists describe it as an "intergenerational phenomena, characterized by both intertemporal and interpersonal dimensions." There are a host of psychological elements that result in a legacy and what it means.

I define legacy as making decisions now that will affect the generations that follow. Legacy is about what you do, who you are, and what you believe in. In the circle diagram, I use the term "Family Legacy," not just "Legacy." Because it matters even more when it's your family name.

Alfred Nobel invented dynamite. In 1888, his brother, Ludvig Nobel, died. Several newspapers mistakenly published their pre-written obituaries about Alfred. According to legend, a French newspaper wrote, "The Merchant of Death is dead. Dr. Alfred Nobel, who became rich by finding ways to kill more people faster than ever before, died yesterday."[1] Alfred was so horrified by this glimpse of how he might be

---

[1] There's an old movie quote that says, "When the legend becomes fact, print the legend." No one to date has been able to verify the use of the specific phrase, "Merchant of Death," but his vilification by the French press is true.

remembered that he donated most of his extraordinary wealth (the equivalent today of about $5 billion dollars) to establishing the Nobel Prize.

Like Alfred Nobel, or Ebenezer Scrooge in Charles Dickens' *A Christmas Carol*, very few of us get to see how we will be remembered by others. What we *can* do is be clear about what we would *like* to have happen, and then work with the people around us to see that it does.

There are dozens, perhaps hundreds, of ways to define "legacy." And dozens, perhaps hundreds, of ways to arrange your business structure, family architecture and governance principles to achieve that legacy. **The best way to ensure that those dreams will come true is to put them all in writing and make sure everyone who will be part of that future knows what it is.** But let's make sure you understand what I mean by "everyone."

> "We may have a dwindling number of candidates in the immediate family. So, the question becomes, do you streamline the business? Maybe sell off certain branches that make it easier to manage, or do you figure out a way to actively recruit more family? Do you think about selling to your employees in an employee stock ownership plan, so it becomes employee-owned and not just limited to one family? We're looking at all of those options." ~ *Jim Phillip, CEO, Phillip's Flowers & Gifts*

Before you can answer which direction you choose, it is critical that you understand who the family members are and what's their perspective about the business and the family members involved in it. When you have a family business you've founded or are working in, you generally think of your legacy as taking care of those family members directly engaged in the business. But there are a lot more folks on the peripheral, especially as generations engage each other. The founding generation (G1) is typically two or four people (say, two brothers or sisters and their spouses) which might make it easy to communicate and get everyone to understand what should happen. G2 gets a little bit bigger (as their children mature) and by G4 it can easily become unmanageable. One family business I work with had less than twenty family members through G3. At G4 that number has nearly doubled, many of whom have no direct connection to the company.

Many clients have family members working in their business. As part of helping them improve the sustainability of their legacy, I ask, "Who is your family?" The answers I get vary, but one typical response is that they name only the family members directly involved in the business.

I follow up with questions about children, grandchildren, spouses, etc., the extended family that may *not* be involved in the business. Even if they're not directly employed in the business, they play an important role in the family legacy. I include those members in surveys about their business and their family in order to understand *all* the needs and emotions that should be considered in the legacy journey. **The successive generations need to be prepared to understand and embrace their stewardship going forward.** As you will see in Chapter 5, there are several important ways to address this. How does a lifetime of work become a legacy? How can successors grow into their legacy?

C-12 is an organization that uses CEO peer groups to create a space for business leaders to share issues, compare solutions, and seek advice to help move their business forward. Tony Tennaro is the head of C-12 in Charlotte, North Carolina. He is a friend of mine and we have discussed ways to help business leaders navigate the issues they face. I have enjoyed advising some of C-12's members on how to engage all of their associates in order to create a culture of respect and results. Tony points out the importance of making sure that all associates of an organization understand the mission, vision, and core values of the business. This is particularly true in family businesses.

"One of the first things we ask every CEO who joins C12 is, "What's your mission, vision, and core values? Is it something you can tell me? Is it something that you know? Don't show me your wall plaque. Can you *tell* me what it is? And if I went into your company, could I ask someone, and they would tell me it as well?"
~ *Tony Tennaro, Principal Chair, C12 Charlotte*

One place to start is to ask yourself—and other family members—a few basic (but not simple) questions:

- Do they understand and support the values of the family?
- Do they have a knowledge of what the company does, its products and communities it serves?
- Do they relate to the employees of your business?
- Do they have a vision for the benefit of future generations?
- How often do you communicate with the extended family?

More often than not, your most common response will be, "Huh...?" or "Oh, yes, that..." Start by asking and answering those questions for yourself, and then everyone else who will be affected by the legacy you want to leave.

Even if you're not going to have 40 people directly involved in the business, or even on a board of directors, if the business has more than one owner, you need to clarify what "ownership" will mean for everyone else. Consider this short list of possibilities, and while you read it, make a note of which ones you relate to:

- Do you want the business to continue?
- Do you want to shift the business to a different market or even a different industry?
- Do you want to split the business in two or more directions?

- Do you want to sell the business?
    - To your heirs?
    - To your employees?
    - To another company?
- Do you want to establish a trust or foundation?
    - If so, what would be its purpose and structure?
- Do you want to sell the business and reinvest in a new legacy element?

Perhaps you want to do a careful mix of a few of those alternatives, like Trey Taylor did in his business:

> "About ten years ago, I took the better part of a year to sit back and ask, 'What are the real defining values that other people would see in us that I can recognize?' Some of which we get right, and some of which we really try but don't seem to nail all the time. Nobody always lives a hundred percent of their values perfectly. I wanted our values statement to be aspirational and to prompt behaviors that would be ingrained in an identity of being, a sense of being. So we came out with 'Be' attitudes. Each of those is phrased as an instruction: Be truthful. Be client focused. Be intrepid. Be abundance minded. Be fun, loving and determined." ~ *Trey Taylor, Managing Director, Taylor Family Office*

Legacy is really about asking and answering the question of what the purpose is going forward, and how will it benefit others? This concept invokes the idea of *stewardship*. You are the steward of the business for the present, and how you execute that stewardship will affect the future of the business and your family. The psychological impact of being a steward can be found in the conversations I have with clients and guests on my podcast.

> "For me, thinking about stewardship means thinking about caring for others. It's a little bit of sublimating

the self. It doesn't mean you don't have fun along the way. It's just means that you are making investments of both of time and resources to support those future generations. When you think of stewardship of land, for example, it could be stewardship of the future generations of trees. For families it could be future generations of children." ~ *Meghan Juday, Chairman of the Board, IDEAL Industries*

It's important to realize it's more than just wealth that gets passed on. Meghan goes on to say:

"When thinking about a family business, not only are you passing on all those wonderful values and wealth and stock and everything else that goes along with it, but you're also passing on any negative disposition you have towards the company or the family. And that can be really devastating. That's one of the things I learned being in our fourth to fifth generations of ownership. Some of the legacy in our family was faulty communication or dysfunctional dynamics that started back in the second generation. So, legacy is two sides of the same coin. If each generation is not careful about the legacy that they're creating and passing down for future generations, you can end up with a very destructive legacy passed along with all the good stuff."

Whatever your idea or plan, it must include the people closest to you and closest to the business.

The simplest way to find out is to *ask*. Communication becomes one of the keys to understanding potential negative feelings about the company or the family members. That understanding can allow you to alter the course of the frustrations or needs of family members to the point where the legacy is primarily positive and sustainable.

Communication processes will change over time with geographical expansion of both the family and the business, with technological developments and other factors. The overriding "filter" for the conversations needs to be the umbrella of your family values and the respect you have for each other's point of view.

Maybe it's a conversation with your current partners. That's easy enough in G1 or G2, but even then, you might need to use a neutral third party to survey everyone and get a sense of what others' expectations are. It's a sound business practice even if you're not a family-owned business. People are always more willing to talk more openly when they know the survey will be anonymous.

I have conducted many surveys over the years. Each case is different, however, in almost every case, the answers to the survey questions revealed surprises that no one expected. More importantly, those "surprises" were significant enough to change assumptions about decisions impacting the business. The surveys have revealed important information about Family members desires to cash out of the business, members who had credible objections to the strategy of the business, members who didn't have any idea of what the vision for the business is, or what the family values are.

Once this information was known, it had a profound impact on the business. Examples of how the information from these surveys have impacted my clients are:

- Change the strategic focus of the business from one large acquisition to a more strategic acquisition that has been completed, integrated into the business, and led to competitive advantage in the marketplace and significant profitable growth.
- The recognition of the need for a liquidity plan to address the retirement needs or withdrawal desires of shareholders in order to prevent such events from leading to a sale or insolvency of the company.
- Engagement of family members in understanding what the business was about in order to keep them connected to and engaged in the business instead of

seeing the business as a means for a payout that would negatively impact the desired legacy.
- Open a dialogue to consider options for growth that were not recognized previously. These options led to pivoting to successful significant growth options.
-

Once you have a clear idea of what you want your legacy to be, you need to bring everyone into alignment.

Communication regarding alignment around the future direction of the business on a regular basis is critical We call it strategic planning. Generational engagement 9discussed in chapter 5) inform strategic planning in ways that increase your ability to achieve your intended legacy. I was discussing this concept with a friend of mine, Steve Lance. He recounted an example of the communication process being used to determine alignment through engagement. They regularly conducted "Branding Interventions" with their clients. They gather key senior people around a conference table and make the group answer basic marketing and planning questions. In the words of one of the consultants:

> "We were doing one of our interventions, and we start each session by asking participants where they see the business in five years. We have them write the answers on index cards, so they aren't influenced at first by other peoples' answers. In this session we had eight attendees, and when the index cards were collected, my partner counted ten cards. We asked the room who added an extra card, and the Founder and CEO sheepishly admitted he wrote three different answers.
>
> "'I'm not sure where I see the business in five years,' he said. 'Some days I think about just closing it and retiring. Sometimes I think about selling it to the team.

Legacy 51

And other times I think about selling to a larger competitor.'

"My partner and I could see the reactions around the table as everyone finally realized why they couldn't get the CEO's approval on any of their long-range initiatives." ~ *Steve Lance, CD & COO, PS Insights*

Creating a legacy can be a way of giving meaning to one's life and, in some cases, people see a legacy as providing a sense of immortality. A problematic aspect of decision making is that the interests of future individuals often conflict with the interests of the current decision makers. Decisions that affect future generations are also affected by how previous generations treated the current generation. In those cases, it's not too late to realize that an old pattern of neglecting the needs of future generations can be broken now through generational engagement.

Legacies are relevant whenever the consequences of one's actions impact future generations. Some of the circumstances that impact the decision to create a legacy to be taken into consideration are:

- The magnitude of the conflict with current decision makers.
- The time between the decision and the future impact.
- The distance between the generation of the current decision makers and the generation(s) of future benefactors.
- The time into the future for the impact to manifest.
- Have previous generations made decisions for the benefit of current generations?
- How do current owners see their mortality?

The graphic of the Elements of Legacy demonstrates how all those questions fit in the diagram between the core of

Family and Business Architecture and the outer circle of Family Legacy.

Each element needs to be addressed, and each is inseparable in its impact on creating a legacy. They do, however, require separate analysis and solutions to maximize their contribution to a positive and sustainable legacy. We'll examine each of these in the following chapters. They're important, whether you intend the legacy to be the continuation of a specific company or if you pivot to use your wealth in some other way to provide a legacy, as did Alfred Nobel. Either way, let your family values be your guiding principle, and always ask yourself, "How do we wish to be remembered?"

Regardless of the shape you want to give your business and legacy, the steps you need to take are the same for everyone:

1. Ask yourself if there is a vision for the future of the family?
2. Ask your partners if they agree or disagree.
3. Develop a way (surveys, interviews, third-party advisors, attorneys) to find out what everyone who will be affected thinks and feels about the business.
4. Bring everyone together and use that knowledge to propose a vision and goal for your family.
5. Put a team in charge of outlining steps that have to happen.
6. Make sure everyone who will be part of that future is involved in the conversations on what must be done.
7. Put it all in writing. A governance plan. A business plan. A succession plan. Every type of plan that your business and family will need.
8. If possible, make the signing of those agreements a family celebration.

Legacy

Let's go back to the Three-Circle Model developed by Renato Tagiuri and John Davis.

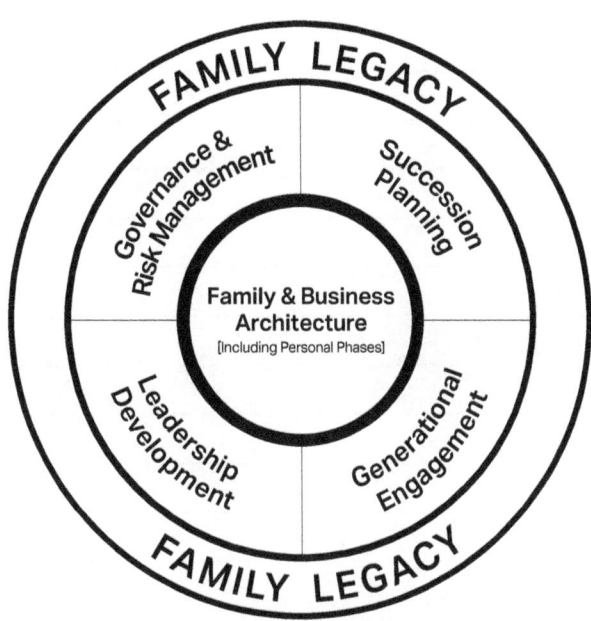

There are seven different ways employees and family members can engage – or not engage – with the business. It's important to include all of them as you outline your plan. Get it right and you're on your way to business growth and family harmony. But if everyone is not in agreement, you should set aside a huge war chest for the legal battles that will follow your passing.

Legacy Thought Starters

Download the 8½ x 11 printable forms from:
ExpertsInHow.com/thought-starters

What do you want your legacy to be?

_____

Does everyone agree with you?

- ☐ Yes
- ☐ No
- ☐ I don't know

If you were to conduct an independent survey of your family business participants, what do you believe you could learn?

_____

What questions would you like them to answer?

_____

Legacy

_____
_____
_____
_____

Using the Three-Circle Model of the Family Business System, identify everyone in each segment:

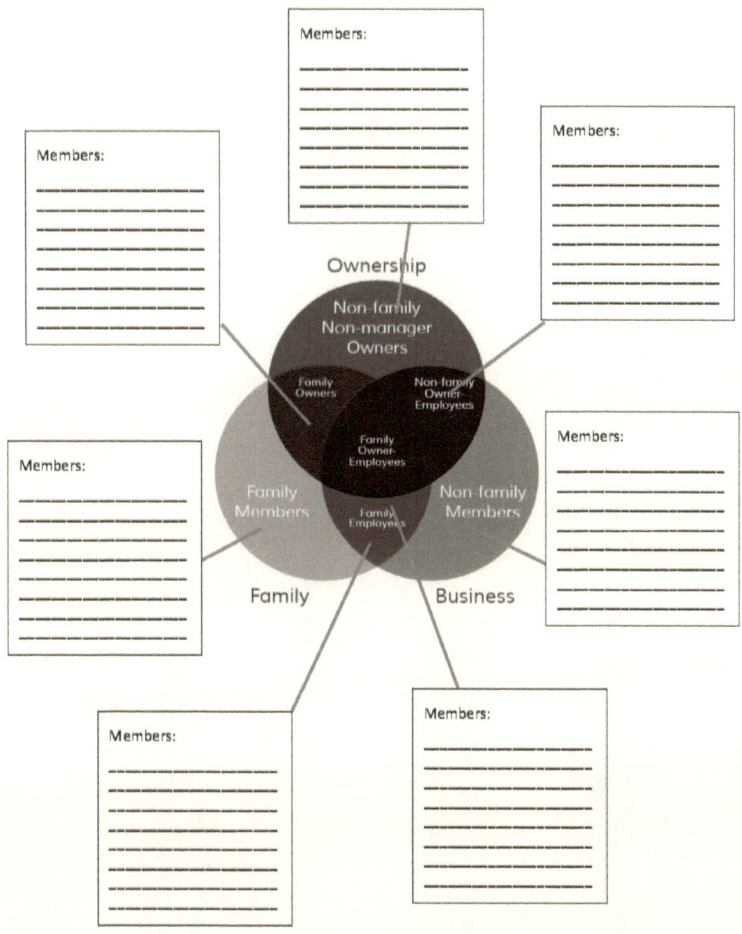

Chapter 4

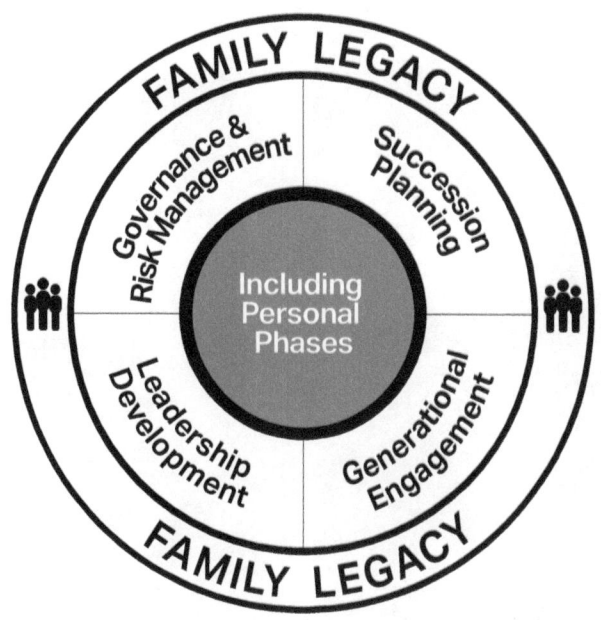

PERSONAL PHASES

"We meet again, at last. The circle is now complete. When I left you, I was but the learner. Now, I am the master."

~Darth Vader to Obi Wan Kenobi, *Star Wars IV*

When a family owns a business, it becomes part of their identity. Just as we all go through different relationship phases as human beings, family business owners go through different phases in their relationship to the business. The importance of this is understanding where the family members are in their journey through their personal phase. When we help clients with this concept it helps them put into perspective the reaction of family members due to their generational phase and their operational phase in the business. When clients gain this understanding, they have been able to have difficult conversations in a more respectful and productive way that allowed them to advance their legacy rather than derail it.

Personal Phases is the term I use for the individual process of learning and growing in different roles as family members advance through their careers. There are four primary stages, and four generational ones:

1. Starting a business

You might have a new idea, like those we see on *Shark Tank*, or you might decide to start your version of an existing business. Whatever your inspiration, there's a good chance that even though you have a product idea, a customer-based idea, or a service idea, entrepreneurs and G1 partners often have no background scaling that idea.. If you have a technical or engineering background, you may even know the process to make that product. Maybe not *many* products, but *that* product. You understand which customer needs you can fill, and if you pick the right one, you begin selling. The next step is to say, "I know this product, I know how it works, and I know how to tell the customer how to make it work, but I've gone from one customer to 50, and now I need more than one of me. I need other people who know what I know, or at least some of what I know."

That entrepreneurial mindset arises out of the knowledge that the founder is one who views decision-making as *their* sole responsibility as the creator, builder, and operator of the business. The expectation is that the vision for the business is theirs, and it's a significant element of why they started the business. In addition, they feel that as the person(s) taking on a greater financial risk it's non-negotiable. Decision making is controlled by the entrepreneur as a centralized process and expected to be done quickly. There's little connection to the idea that decision making is another term for governance. But in order to grow, the founder(s) need to move to the second stage:

2. Managing a business

Every family member who becomes part of the business needs to understand how that business runs, and how to run that business. Founders often have a hard time with this because they started the business with a passion for what the business *does*, not a passion for how the business *runs*. As founder, we must learn how to manage other people to help do what you do, since one person can't do everything. In general, and not just in family-owned businesses, people will tell you that **managing people is the hardest part, and it's a different skill from starting and growing a business.** Also, the process of management can often be cold, logical, and fact-based. But surprise! When you start managing people, you've got all the emotional elements that come along with it. You must learn how to engage with people to get the best out of them. Then you must be aware what attributes you're looking for. You need to understand how they're going to relate to customers, learn the product, the manufacturing process, and any of a thousand other skills.

This requires developing a strong team and trusting others to handle important tasks. It can be difficult for founders to let go of control, but it's necessary to focus on strategy and planning. With many clients, we help them with the need for establishing succession planning and a governance structure which allows the founder to maintain control over significant decisions, which lets the founder(s) evolve to:

3. Owning the business

In this phase I am referring to stepping away from day-to-day management. Now you need a more Olympian overview, and this is where governance becomes crucial. Will the managers you've hired to run the day-to-day know all the smart ways to serve your customers? To get to Owner you need to know what a Balance Sheet looks like and what it means to the business. You do not need to understand accounts payable or accounts receivable as much as you need to understand cash flows. You need to understand the timing of working capital and other technical aspects that go along with it.

When the founder, or future generations of the family, transition from a managerial role to an ownership role, they must focus on the bigger picture and prioritize long-term planning, financial management, and governance. Succession planning and a good governance structure become more important than ever. In addition, generational engagement will play a big role in the ability of the family to connect ownership with the family governance structure and the business governance structure to maintain appropriate control of the business, and influence over its direction.

It can be difficult for any of us to step away and let someone else take care of our "baby", our most important asset, our legacy!

As an Owner, you must discern the level of governance you can rely on, let them do their job, and not get in their way, while staying informed about what's going on so you can influence decisions that follow your goals, your family values, your perspective for customer service, your perspective for product quality, and on and on.

I see many clients who don't realize the importance of engaging *all* generations of the family in understanding the business, its products, its associates, its communities of customers and vendors, and its role in allowing individuals of progressive generations to pass through the phases in ways that allow family legacies to continue. Megan Juday describes how it takes and understanding of the business and what it means to the family to inform the journey of your legacy.

> "I grew up talking about Ideal. My father was CEO for a long time and then became chairman. But as I started working for the family on behalf of the company and started thinking about how we get this company down to the next generation, I started noticing a strong sense of legacy in our family. We want to do the right things for future generations." ~ *Meghan Juday, Chairman of the Board, IDEAL Industries*

Often an ownership role for the family takes on a more remote role than making day-to-day decisions. The founder may be more remote from the company, the geographic location of family owners may mean they're remote from the business locations as well. This provides an opportunity to establish a long-term strategy for family engagement in the business and ensure its continued success towards the desired legacy, which leads you to:

4. Investor

Your active relationship with the company might stop at Board Chair along the way, and then become a pure investor. This is another step with a new set of challenges. It's a step where you're now in the process of not just being the owner of a business, you're looking to invest, or advise other families on investing in the businesses. This is sometimes known as the

Personal Phases

family office approach. Now you have to think about the company from the point of view of what you look for in a business you might acquire or might advise somebody else to acquire. By now, you might have a portfolio of companies. All this can take place over a significant arc of time. If you're G1 and created the business, you've likely put your entire life into it. And even successive generations might be family members who have worked with the company 20, 30, 40 years or more. It's a huge challenge to let go and step away.

Finally, as the founder or current family owners' transition from an ownership role into an investment role, you must learn to let go of control and focus on your *investments* in the business rather than its *operations*. This can be an emotional experience, as the family may have deep ties to the business, its associates, and the communities they serve. However, it's also an opportunity to diversify investments and explore new opportunities to potentially pivot the family wealth in a new direction and a new chapter of their legacy.

If someone is unwilling or unable to go through any one of those phases, the chances of the company failing as a legacy increase over time. There's a direct relationship between going through those phases and building a successful legacy. The journey through these personal phases is not just related to the founder (G1), it's a journey for each generational family member who has an equity stake in the business. Even if you're not the founder, chances are excellent that you'll face *all* those phases, and these generational challenges as well:

5. Evolving the business

The world is changing, and successful companies need to adapt. The quote from Jamie Shyer in the Introduction was part of a longer story he told on my podcast. His father and uncle (G2) understood they needed to change the way their company manufactured eyewear. They recognized it was the only way to successfully compete. While Jamie's grandfather may have started the business, the next generation had to adapt.

What Bill McLean talked about in the Overview was that his father recognized the time was right to open a new location, something Bill's grandfather thought was ridiculous. So even if you're not the G1 founder, you'll probably face a crossroads where the business must change to survive.

6. Pivoting the business

Whether it was the Rockefeller family, or Trey Taylor's story of shifting his family's primary business to philanthropy, every aspect of the business needs to be re-thought, top-to-bottom. Do you have the right people for the new company? Who do you need? Do family members have the knowledge, experience and understanding to make the new business thrive? All of that becomes part of another personal phase.

7. Stepping up or stepping in

An unexpected death in the family can mean an unplanned shift in management for both the company and the family. Who's ready? Who's not? Has your succession plan prepared you for this, not just legally, but professionally?

In the next chapter on Generational Engagement, I'll talk about this in much more depth. It's another example of why generational engagement should start as early as possible. That doesn't mean a classroom set up with five-year-olds sitting there trying to understand the engineering drawings. It means making sure family members know each other and understand who their cousins and aunts and uncles are. If the decision must be made for one of them to take over in an emergency, and nobody knows each other or their needs, there's likely to be a fight. The fact that people understand these things, and there's been some stock taken in terms of who's even *interested* in going forward as a leader, if and when that happens, even if it's on an interim basis, letting other people know *who* that is and *why*, is critically important.

If your family has a strong Leadership Development program in place, it can make this phase, and the next, as easy as possible:

8. Joining the business

At some point, every family member is going to be "new" to the business. Whether it's working the sales floor as a summer intern, coming on board as a new college graduate, returning to the family business after another career, inheriting a non-participatory ownership share, or marrying into the family. Your family council needs to have thought through a specific onboarding process for each of those scenarios. Without a plan, the chances of the business failing will increase exponentially.

While all eight of those phases present risks, at the bottom line, family-owned, family-run businesses have several unique opportunities. For example, they often have a strong sense of tradition and family values that can provide the glue that holds the family and the business together. They also can develop strong relationships with employees and customers, which can help build a loyal customer base and attract top talent, all of which can create a competitive advantage. Bill McLean was discussing the strength of family's impact on business during an episode of my podcast. He said:

> "Family business owners are individuals who don't look at a job as a job. They look at it as an absolute commitment to the communities they operate in, to the employees and the families they support. As a function of that, the concept of legacy to them matters enormously in terms of what events and actions they've taken that leaves this lasting impact well beyond the time that they're at the business." ~ *Bill McLean, Partner, Richter*

In more than 40 years managing and advising family businesses, I've seen that family-owned, family-run businesses face a unique set of challenges and opportunities as the founder transitions from an entrepreneurial role to a managerial, ownership, and investment role. For example, what do you do if a family member is heading in the right direction, but is not quite ready? Do you recruit an outsider knowing that person is just an interim placeholder? How do you assuage the feelings of the family member who is being told, "You're not ready?" That's just one aspect to address, and there's no "one-size-fits-all" answer. It comes down to an understanding of what the business and the family need.

By recognizing these challenges and opportunities, and working to develop the necessary skills and mindset, founders and subsequent generations can navigate each of these transitions successfully and ensure the long-term success of their family business to achieve their desired legacy.

I've been fortunate to be involved in successful transition of family businesses at Rust-Oleum, Rand McNally, Blyth, and others. Developing relationships is the key to that success.

Personal Phases Thought Starters

Download the 8½ x 11 printable forms from: ExpertsInHow.com/thought-starters

Use the following grid to ask and answer these questions:
1. What phase do you believe you are at?
    Starting a business
    Managing a business
    Owning a business
    Investor
    Evolving the business
    Pivoting the business
    Stepping up or stepping in
    Joining the business
2. What phase do you believe the CEO is at?
3. Are you ready to move to the next phase?
4. When will you be ready, and who will take over your old role?
5. What skill(s) do you have to add or let go of to move to the next phase?
6. Who can help you do that?

Family Member	Phase they're in	Phase that comes next	When will they be ready?
YOU			

Chapter 5

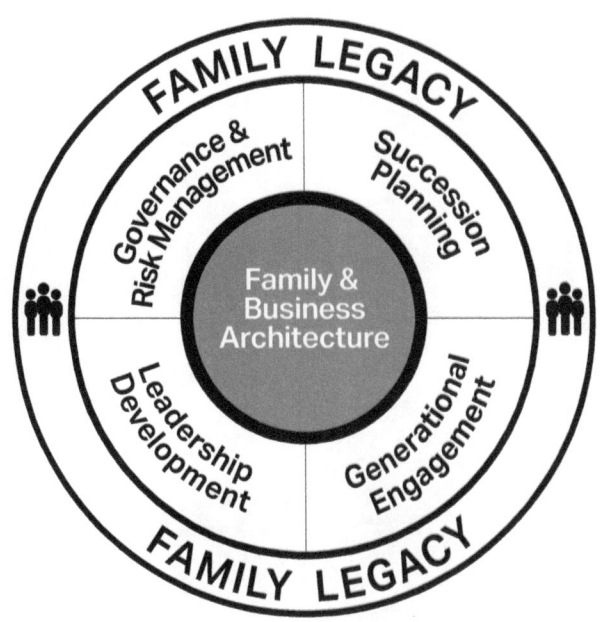

FAMILY AND BUSINESS ARCHITECTURE

"Do people think that you got your position just because you're family? Or do they think you're actually deserving. My father has always said, when you're in a family business, you work twice as hard, and get half the credit."

~Ashley D. Joyce, Chair, The Duchossois Family Foundation

Family dynamics can have either a positive or negative impact on the business. When family members work together, personal conflicts can quickly spill over into the workplace. Family relationships can also create bias and favoritism, which can impact how decisions are made.

A significant challenge of family-owned businesses comes when they're run more like a family than like a business. This can be good in some ways; it can create a sense of loyalty and shared purpose. However, it can also lead to a lack of discipline and structure. The structure, or architecture, works best when there is an established formal decision-making process. Ideally, all constituents are represented in the decision-making process; a select group of family members, and a group representing the business. This can be either a senior leadership team or Board of Directors. Again, let me emphasize that there is not a "one size fits all" solution, and it's important to develop an architecture that works best for your family and your business. Most important, the Family and Business **architecture that works best will likely change as both your family and business evolve**.

Clearly the relationship between family and the business is important. The other relationship dynamic at work is the one *between* family members, whether the members are working in the business or not. One of the biggest challenges is balancing business needs with family relationships. As I've stated earlier, most experts agree that business needs should come *first* to build a lasting legacy that provides for the family for generations to come. But "comes first" does not, or should not mean, "comes instead." It's vitally important for the health of the business and the health of the family that members who are part of the business know to leave work at the office when they come home.

The concept of "team" applies to the family as well as other forms of organizations. I've had the pleasure of having two people in particular as podcast guests who shared their experience as members of teams at the highest level of competition in their respective sports. Sherry Winn is a two-time Olympian and former NCAA coach of the year in basketball. Phil Wellington was an all American in college, played in Major League Soccer, and played for the US men's national team in soccer. An important lesson came out of our discussion. They not only understood their role as leaders with their ability, but they also understood their role as leaders in supporting and respecting their teammates who may have had less talent than they did. So too is the case in families. Some members have more or less skill and experience than others. Supporting and respecting each member is critical to building and sustaining an architecture that works.

> "As a coach, it's your responsibility to coach teams to collaborate—the art of giving and receiving. These are the same principles that you use in business. It's about the team first, and your capacity to enable those people to work together. The ability to work together comes down to cooperation, which comes down to respect and trust, which comes down to the ways you interact and treat people.]" ~ *Sherry Winn, Two-Time Olympian, CEO, The Winning Leadership Company. Author of Winning Leadership: Seven Secrets to Being a Truly Powerful Leader*

> "You can choose from respecting yourself, respecting the people around you, respecting your family, and respecting the people who work with you when you use words like "family" and "business." They're already emotionally charged. How do you show respect for their positions without escalating the emotional charge

Family and Business Architecture

another degree? How do you bring the situation calm?"
~ *Phil Wellington, VP, GM, Siemens Healthineers, former professional athlete*

Putting the business first can create tension between family members. That's why it's so important to pay attention to the family architecture and engage as many generations as possible. Consider the impact it should have on both succession planning, and developing the family architecture that fits best.

My experience with dealing with architectural solutions for several family-owned businesses has revealed a standard framework that can be flexible in its complexity yet covers the critical bases you need in place to ensure success in building your legacy.

Let's take another look at the three-circle diagram of family and business architecture you saw in the Overview:

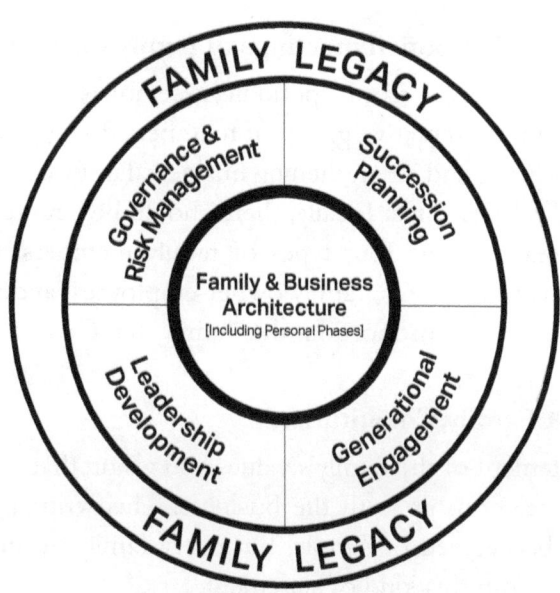

The single most challenging issue related to the interaction of the family and business architecture is the structure and processes for governance of the family itself.

Managing and mastering your family governance depends on creating and maintaining three critical components:

1. **Periodic assemblies of the family (usually once or twice per year).**

If you don't communicate, your family business will start to suffer. Nature—and families—abhor a vacuum. Members who are not actively engaged in the business start to wonder what's happening. If you don't stay in touch, it's human nature to imagine their own version of what's going on. You can't start these gatherings too soon. They can be as simple as a family picnic or reunion. They can start with the younger children (4 years and up) playing games together and advancing over time to as the generations get older (18years and up) to being exposed to tours of business locations and summary presentation about the business.

2. **Family Council meetings of family members.**

This is separate from "periodic assemblies." A Family Council is a representative group of members doing planning, creating policies, and strengthening business-family communication and relationships. Ideally, there should be a representative from each of the four types of family members: family members, family owners, family owner-employees, and family employees, in any proportion the family feels comfortable with.

3. **A Family Constitution.**

A statement of the family's values and vision that regulate members' relationship with the business. This written document can be detailed or simple, but every family in business can benefit from this kind of statement.

In rare cases, you may need a more elaborate family structure with separate meetings of family shareholders. I

Family and Business Architecture

recommend the simplest structure that supports those three components of Periodic Assemblies, Family Council Meetings and a Family Constitution.

When you have decided upon and implemented an appropriate structure, the Family Council and family meetings should focus on three key activities:

- Develop clarity on roles, rights, and responsibilities for family members.
- Encourage family members, family employees, and family owners to act responsibly toward the business and the family.
- Maintain appropriate family and owner inclusion in business discussions.

If the family consists of ten or fewer members (I'm referring to the entire family including in-laws and children) you may not need a formal family council. You could get by discussing in-depth issues at a more informal family gathering. If you have more than ten, I believe families will benefit from a more formal family council structure, with a select group of members who have responsibility to perform certain duties.

It's important for the family council to perform some or all the following duties:

- Keep the family informed about current business, ownership, and family issues and direction.
- Help the family reach decisions and speak with a unified voice about its goals.
- Act as liaison between the family and the company, or a board of directors, if you have one.
- Guard against family interference with the business while seeing that the family's key goals are satisfied.
- Encourage generational engagement.
- Monitor and address family harmony.

A family council can be formed in several ways. The typical way is to have one member of each branch of the family elected to the council. It's important to have representation of all generations, all genders, in-laws, active and passive owners, hometown, and geographically distant relatives where possible.

To address these issues, many family-owned businesses have adopted a board of advisors or a board of directors. The role of the board is to provide objective advice and guidance to the family members and non-family members in management who are running the business. The board can also provide an outside perspective and help to keep the family members and management accountable.

The composition of the board is critical to its effectiveness. It's important to have a mix of family and non-family members on the board to provide a diversity of perspectives. It's also important to have individuals with a variety of skills and experience, such as finance, marketing, and operations.

The typical structure of the family council will interact with the business through this board of directors or a board of advisors. If there is no board, then the family council would interact with the business through the management team. As described, the family council sets policy for the family, the board of directors, board of advisors, or senior management sets policy for the business. The two structures should coordinate their work in the form of governance policies and procedures.

As you've probably noticed, this question of family structure and business structure is the most complex, and probably the most individualized part of running a family-owned, family-run business, but it must be addressed. The sooner you do it, the better off your family and your business will be in the long run.

Family and Business Architecture

Family And Business Architecture Thought Starters

Download the 8½ x 11 printable forms from:
ExpertsInHow.com/thought-starters

Do you have a family council or organization that's different from the business structure?   Y/N

Do you have a Board of Directors or a Board of Advisors? Y/N

FAMILY COUNCIL REPRESENTATION

Role in the business	Represented (Y/N)	How or by whom?
Owner-Employees		
Owners		
Family Employees		
Family Members		

Some critical questions about communication that affect the effectiveness of your family or business architecture:

- How does the family communicate its desires or expectations to the management of your company?
- Do you feel that the communication between the family and the business is open and respectful?
- Do you believe that members of the family feel that they have an opportunity for their voice to be heard?
- Do you have effective family employment and development policies and processes?

Chapter 6

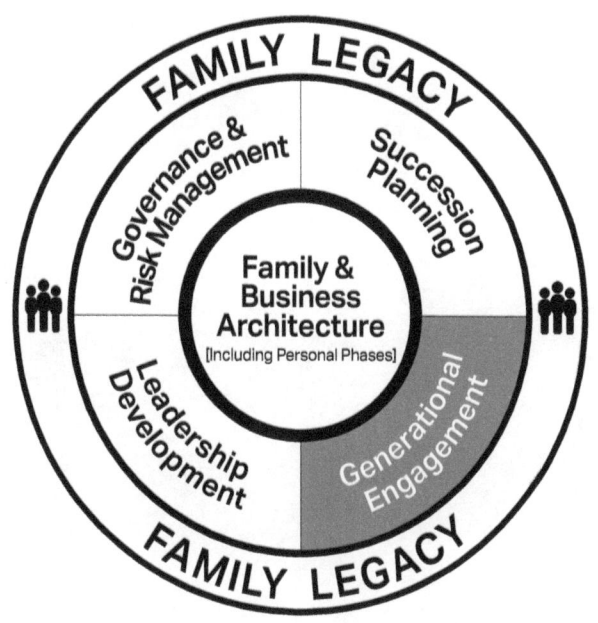

GENERATIONAL ENGAGEMENT

"The best way for family business leaders to prepare the next generation for tomorrow is to help them be successful today."

Generational engagement is one of the foundational elements of creating a legacy. When a family owns a business, that business becomes part of their family as well. It's part of their identity, regardless of where they are in the spectrum of generations. We've all heard someone say, "I am not what I do for a living." You never hear owners of family businesses say that. Their business *is* part of their identity, it's part of their livelihood. It's who they are and how they want to be seen. The degree of generational engagement can vary widely. Some of them represent warning sign that could jeopardize your desired family legacy. A colleague, Bill Goodspeed, put it this way:

> "There are lots of extremes to family engagement. There's the family that has *no* engagement, where the next generation doesn't really care about the business, and they just want the money. Those types of businesses are usually not long for the world, at least not long for the world as a family business. There are those where *everybody* in the family works for the company. And those businesses will have a different set of problems because there's too much family engagement, there's too much involvement, and often destructive nepotism. The ones that work well are the ones that go in the middle of those two extremes where they have family engagement at each generation *and* the board of directors, caring shareholders, and often family executives." ~ *William Goodspeed, Board Chair & Independent Director*

If current generations want to keep that going, other family members must understand what that identity is, and what it means. And it starts with what the family values were when the business started, and what they are today. Several clients and colleagues share their perspective in the following quotes. The remarkable consistency among all of their perspectives is the importance of family values.

> "As long as you hold true to your core values, even in challenging situations, people are going to respect you. When others see that you have unwavering values and act accordingly, you cultivate an environment of trust and reliability." ~ *Ashley D. Joyce, Chair, The Duchossois Family Foundation*

"I think our faith might have been an underlying factor that kind of keeps us together in unified values as well as just, you know, in our business." ~ *Jim Phillip, CEO, Phillip's Flowers & Gifts*

"In our family, we have family values and that makes it easy to make decisions." ~ *Meghan Juday, Chairman of the Board, IDEAL Industries*

"One of the first things we ask every CEO is, 'What's your mission, vision, and core values? Is it something you can tell me?'" ~ *Tony Tennaro, Principal Chair, C12 Charlotte*

"To me, from a legacy perspective with my family, it's living that out and doing the right things that are associated with my faith." ~ *David Judson, Founder & CEO, JRR Solutions*

"Studies have shown [family businesses] are actually more competitive. One of the main reasons is that the families' values are instilled in the business." ~ *William Goodspeed, Board Chair & Independent Director*

The way a family's values get expressed through the business says as much about the family as it does about the business. You might want to help people by creating value. That gets translated into the highest quality products or the highest quality service you can deliver. That knowledge helps

Generational Engagement

employees and family members understand that quality is an element that needs to be preserved. Then, if someone comes in and says, "Here's how we cut costs with cheaper materials," you know immediately that it's not going to work. (Not that it ever does.)

It's an element of making sure the family values get transferred through generations. And if you want to communicate those values to future generations, you must go beyond just the family members who work directly within the business.

I encourage clients to truly identify who has a stake in the business. You need to understand who all those people are: cousins, aunts, uncles, grandchildren, relatives by marriage, all of them. And you must reach out to all those people to get their understanding of what's going on, what they think about the business, what they think about where the business is going, how they feel about the family, what they think about their interest in the business, or do they even know the business exists, as crazy as that may sound. Even though they're not currently shareholders, in management, or on a board, they're likely to be some kind of equity holder or expect to benefit from the equity of the business in the future.

> "It's a little bit uncomfortable at first for people who have never gone through [generational engagement] to think down to that level. We've been doing this for so long. We've had kids and cousin's kids go through swimming lessons together, go to their first trip to Disneyland, visit the graves of their grandparents. All those things are intentionally done to add to the definition and the identity of the people who participate.
>
> "If you do not keep everyone informed, there will come a day when equity falls in their lap and they will say, "Look at this!" and see big dollar signs. "We should sell the company." They have no idea who the communities are that the company serves. What impact that statement will have on all the communities, the people who work there, other family members,

loyal customers, and on and on. You do not want someone to make that decision, or any decision, without that knowledge. *That's* what I mean by Generational Engagement, and why I believe it has to start as early as possible." ~ *Trey Taylor, Managing Director, Taylor Family Office*

It should start when the kids are about four or five years old. Family gatherings should be intentional and regularly scheduled. It doesn't have to be four times a year, but at least annually. Make sure the youngest kids attend so they can play together. They're not there to have a lesson or a presentation on the business or the engineering design of the product, at least not yet. But they gather to start to learn about the personalities, traits, desires and needs of other family members.

It starts with everyone asking, "Who are you? Whose son or daughter, are you? How are we related to each other?" That's the simplest level of involvement. For others, it might mean they're children of the owners or the current CEO, so they grow up hearing stories about the needs and concerns of the company.

Not every child is going to grow up to be the CEO or have a company officer as a parent. It's crucial that the entire family give thought to how those outliers get the exposure they need.

There should be a Family Planning book. Not when the next generation is four or five years old, but for future years, long before they go to college, decide on a major, or decide whether or not they want to be part of the business. Plant visits. Take Your Niece to the Corner Office Day, company location visits, and as they get older, presentations by the senior management team, once, maybe twice a year, on what's going on. Include mentorships, internships, and sitting in on discussions about the business where appropriate.

Another good family architecture tool is the Family Council. It's a mashup of a governing board, a family on-boarding method, or just a follower or fan base. Any way you construct it, the idea is to bring along every and all family members, so they feel part of the business. Communicate, communicate, communicate.

I've seen a number of situations when it comes to generational engagement and have assisted clients to reconsider their engagement perspective and processes to improve family member interest, participation in decision making, and direct the business towards a shared vision and legacy.

My first step in working with a new client is to assess their level of communication and how far that communication extends. In many cases the family members in charge of the business have not considered the need to engage other family members of their own generation, let alone those of newer generations. I encourage them to identify everyone who might be even *distantly* affected by the business, and then I include each of them in a survey about the business and the family. At the end of this chapter, you'll find a sample questionnaire that I give clients to use. I want to know what everyone knows, thinks, believes, and feels. I also want to know what their thoughts and feelings are towards the family and the business.

Too often, core family members involved in the business have a bit of a chip on their shoulders. They may feel that other family members are not capable of contributing to the governance of the business or governance of the family. They may feel they're putting in all the effort, and sometimes that results in attitudes like, "We run it, you don't. So shut up."

That form of family management is a recipe for trouble. And often, when I share the results of the survey (the "what they said" part, not the "who said what" part) management is often surprised by the good thinking that they were not aware of, or by how they are perceived by their own family. We see responses like, "I would join the company if it wasn't so poorly run," reflect concerns about where the business is headed, or "I think they should…" or, "I would love to be part of the company, but I loathe Uncle Bill." These reflect concerns about some family members. In any event, it's imperative to give a voice to those feelings and potential areas for improvement that may have been silent to the detriment of the family and the business.

Those surveys are the raw material of good family dynamics. In research we call it Qualitative Analytics—the subjective attitudes that are part of the family dynamic. Identifying and understanding these attitudes is critical to putting together an effective and productive generational engagement process.

After taking a survey of the attitudes and opinions of the entire family, one common starting point is to give the family members an understanding of governance principles, for both family governance and business governance.

A listing and explanation of the skills needed to run or advise the business can help family members understand what's required. I helped clients draft the communication to next generation members of a family to help that next generation understand what governance is about, and what their roles in governance might be. The letter describes the skills that are required by the business and the sets of skills needed that relate to family members who would be selected to be part of business decision-making.

Business Skills

One is a technical skill set, which most family members will not likely have based on their experience, chosen career paths, age, and so on. If you only put that information on paper and ask, "What do you think?" they will likely be uncomfortable, not know how to answer, and will, by human nature feel that they're not qualified to participate in the business. This situation will cause many family members to avoid engaging in the business.

If the future generations decide to drop out of the process, then you'll have lost that important connection to their input, values, and ability to direct the business in a meaningful way to

Generational Engagement

create a legacy. The next scene in that sad movie is a sale or dissolution of the business.

Relationship Skills

The second, and equally important set of skills are those from the family relationship side. The skills needed here lead to questions like, "Do you have the trust of the family?" "Do you feel you can disagree with the family members and still move forward in other areas?" "Do you understand the family values, and do you believe in them?" These are all questions I take families through to help them understand where they are in the generational engagement process.

Communication and respect

Remember the introductory comment, "Stop the screaming!" For many families that's a very real and very big issue. Some families can move past it. In my podcast interview with Jamie Shyer, he talked about how his family would fight like hell about things at work, and then when they sat down for Thanksgiving dinner said, "We need to be civil to one another. We don't have to like everything everybody thinks, but we must learn how to be polite and respectful of one another."

Generational engagement keeps family-owned, family-run business young, vibrant and growing. It's no secret that younger people often have different priorities and interests than their parents and grandparents, and it's essential to find ways to keep them engaged and involved.

Education

The next step in the engagement process is education. Education about what the purpose of the business is, the key strategic issues, the products, the associates, and the communities the business serves.

One effective way to engage younger generations in education is to involve them in decision-making. By giving them a say in the direction of the business, you not only show that you value their opinions, but you also help ensure that the business remains relevant and adaptable to changing times. Could a 70-year-old patriarch pivot a retail company into e-commerce? Unlikely. Could a 30-year-old manager show a business how to move to a global digital platform? Probably. When young people feel they have a stake in the future, they're more likely to be invested in its success.

Another key to engaging younger generations is to provide opportunities for growth and development within the company. This could mean offering mentorship or training programs, or creating new roles or departments that align with their interests and strengths. These programs could include guided site visits to offices, warehouses, manufacturing facilities, etc., presentations by senior management about key areas of the business, or non-voting roles in decision making bodies such as the board of directors. By showing younger generations that there's room for growth and advancement, you can help to foster a sense of loyalty and commitment.

One tool used by companies that have a Board of Directors or Board of Advisors is the role of "Associate: Director". Ashely Joyce, Chair of the Duchossois Family Foundation, described to me in an interview for my book The Power of Respect in Business, how their family company utilized this approach to great success including her rise to Chair the family foundation. I've been involved in the implementation of this type of role for family business as a means for leadership development and generational engagement. It teaches next generation members what governance is all about, respectful interactions with others even if there is disagreement, managing risk., and the responsibility of ownership.

As you get each generation engaged, be clear to establish roles and responsibilities for each family member involved in the business. This helps to ensure that everyone is on the same page, so there's no confusion about who is responsible for

Generational Engagement

what. By clearly defining roles and responsibilities, you can prevent or mitigate conflicts and misunderstandings.

Family dynamics can be complex, and it's not always easy to navigate the various personalities and relationships. By being willing to adjust and adapt as needed, you can help to ensure that everyone feels valued and heard.

At the end of the day, the key to generational engagement is to create a culture of collaboration, open communication, and mutual respect. By providing a voice for *all* family members, and valuing everyone's opinions and contributions, you can help to ensure that the business remains successful for many years to come.

A business that can't get there is unlikely to succeed. Family businesses that can't get there won't succeed either. Generational engagement is critical because it informs succession planning, builds awareness of governance practices, and contributes to leadership development.

Generational Engagement Thought Starters

Download the 8½ x 11 printable forms from: ExpertsInHow.com/thought-starters

Do you have appropriate programs for identifying and developing future leaders of your business?

Here's a checklist of skill sets to consider when creating a development plan for engaging future generations for participation in the business, either as Management, Directors, or Owners. Do your future generations have:

- ☐ Knowledge of your business, what the products are, who the customers are, who your associates are, and the communities you serve.
- ☐ An understanding of and strong belief in your family values.
- ☐ The ability to effectively communicate the needs of the family to the business leaders.
- ☐ The ability to handle discussions with people who have significantly more experience.
- ☐ Financial acumen.
- ☐ Strategic planning experience.
- ☐ Other technical skills appropriate for your business.

Here's an example questionnaire to find out what family members think and feel about your family business. It would be customized of course to fit a specific business and specific issues that the business might be facing. **I cannot stress enough how important it is to have a third party** (not a family member or company executive) **send out the questionnaire and compile the answers.**

Example Survey Questionnaire

The objective of this survey is to collect the thoughts of the adult members of the (NAME OF FAMILY) family about (Company name). **Your responses will be kept confidential.** Please submit your response by (date) directly to (outside consultant). The email address to send your reply is (consultant email address) or text smartphone photos of completed pages to (phone number).

Personal perspective

What interest do you personally have in the family business?

What do you know about how the company and/or family make decisions about the business?

What do you feel you know about the company, its products, communities it serves, etc.?

Are you interested in having a role in the business, now or in the future?

As a member of the family that owns (company name), what would you do with the business if you were the sole owner?

What is your overall impression of the company?

Business performance

How do you feel about the performance of the business?

How would you rate the performance of the business on a scale of 1 to 5 (with 5 being excellent, 3 being acceptable, and 1 being unacceptable)? Please explain your answers.

Operationally _____

Customer Engagement _____

Products _____

Professionalism/Service _____

Diversity _____

What changes would you make in the way the business is run today?

What does the business do well?

What does the business need to do better?

Industry perspective

What industry trends do you see having a major impact on the business in the near term (3 to 5 years) and long term (5 years plus)?

What do you see as the future of the company's products?

What do you see as the future of the company's competitors?

All of this is information, input and insight can guide the family management and business management teams going forward.

Chapter 7

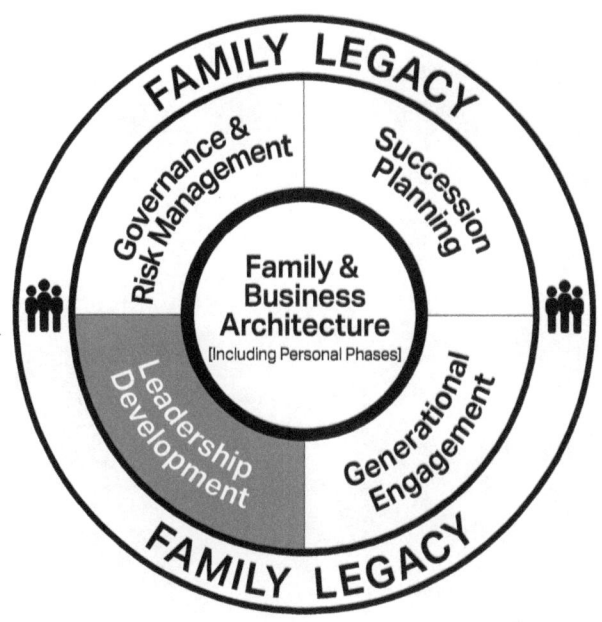

LEADERSHIP DEVELOPMENT

CEO: "It's a waste of money to invest in training. What if we *train* them and they *leave?*"

Head of HR: "What if we *don't* train them, and they *stay?*"

Beyond Generational Engagement, one of the biggest challenges that families face is developing leadership experience and skills for family members and creating meaningful opportunities for the successors to actually lead the family *and* the business.

A lot has been written about leadership and leadership development. My definition of leadership places an equal emphasis on results and relationships. When it comes to results, there are many examples of what to measure, and how to monitor the state of the business. There are financial statements, productivity ratios, KPI's, and performance against benchmarks. But when it comes to relationships, there are few objective ways to measure success.

I wrote a book on leadership titled *The Power of Respect in Business*. In it there are numerous stories depicting relationship encounters. Stories of my own experiences as well as stories of other leaders' experiences are included. The overriding need for leaders to be aware of is the need to establish relationships. For many of us the "how" to create and foster relationships is not something we learn from a class. It comes through your own experience and sharing the experiences of others.

When it comes to leadership development in family business, there are unique challenges and opportunities that require a different approach than what you might find in non-family businesses. I've worked with numerous family businesses over the years, and I have seen firsthand the importance of managing emotions, communication, respect in relationships, and clarity in achieving success.

Managing Emotions

Family businesses are inherently emotional, and that's not always a bad thing. Emotions can be a powerful driver of passion, commitment, and loyalty. However, emotions can also lead to conflict, tension, and misunderstandings. That's why it's essential for family business leaders to learn how to manage their emotions effectively.

> "Do they have emotional intelligence and discipline? Do they treat the people in the mailroom the same as they treat the people in the boardroom? With consistency and respect all the time? You can't do it part of the time because that's how leaders lose respect." ~ *Phil Wellington, VP, GM, Siemens Healthineers*

"Sometimes it's good to have it out, have a good fight, then make up and go on." ~ *Jim Phillip, CEO, Phillip's Flowers & Gifts*

In thinking about emotions, I developed an "emotional scale" in my previous book on leadership. The scale is not clinical, rather it's a scale related to experiences. The key point about the emotional scale is that:

- We are *somewhere* on an emotional scale *all* the time.
- It's important for each of us to learn our own emotional scale and be able to recognize its stages.
- It's most important to learn what triggers each of us to move up or down our own emotional scale.

How we display our emotions is key to building relationships in general, but specifically with those with whom we disagree. If we learn how to recognize our emotional triggers and manage them effectively, we have the greatest chance to lead effectively. It's not always about being *right*; it's about being *effective*. Tina Greenbaum is a colleague and an expert in the psychology of self-awareness. She described the challenge of emotions.

> "We can't change what we're not aware of. People use data and analysis and numbers, and they can see what's working and what's not working. If we don't do that for ourselves, then we're walking around blind. I always say that everybody knows your blind spots, wouldn't you want to know them as well?" ~ *Tina Greenbaum, CEO, Mastery Under Pressure*

In addition, one of the most critical things family business leaders should do is to separate their personal relationships from their professional ones. It's not always easy, but it's essential to be able to put aside personal disagreements and focus on what's best for the business. Leaders must also learn how to communicate effectively and respectfully, even in emotionally charged situations.

Communication

Clear communication is one of the most critical leadership factors in the success of any business, and it's no different in family businesses. Effective communication helps build trust, avoid misunderstandings, and ensure that everyone is working towards the same goals. Clear, respectful, effective communication leads to accountability. It's shared accountability. Walter Davis founded and manages his family business. He's effective because he understands shared accountability.

> "At the end of the day, someone says, 'I'm accountable.' But in that accountability, I'm also accountable to hearing from all those that I need to hear from: different voices and a different side of the argument that might change my mind. Even though I have that dominant behavior, I'm able to say, "Okay, let me listen to something different now." ~ *Walter Davis, Founding Member, Peachtree Providence Partners*

Family business leaders should strive to be open and honest in their communication, even when it's difficult. They should also be willing to listen to different perspectives and ideas, even if they don't agree. By fostering a culture of open communication, family businesses can ensure that everyone is working towards the same goals. An example of how to improve communication skills is to "listen longer." When someone approaches you with a situation, if you're thinking about the solution while they're talking, you're not really listening to them, and they can tell. Even if your thoughts are intended to be helpful, there are several effects of not truly listening while someone is trying to describe a problem.

- As I mentioned, people will feel that you are not listening, and you will lose the ability to build trust.
- If you listen long enough, you may find that where you thought they were going with the discussion was not in fact where they were going, and you find yourself talking about a solution that is not correct.

By listening longer, people will recognize when you're listening to them and that you care about what they're saying, and you will build the trust that will lead to the relationship that allows you to focus on results when leading and organization (whether that organization is your family or your business). Kim Adele-Randall is an experienced leadership consultant in the United Kingdom. I met her through mutual contacts and I was a guest on her podcast discussing what I call the leadership of respect.

> "When somebody's talking, we immediately decide, 'Oh, I think they're right. I think they're wrong. I think they're this, I think they're that.' I try to suspend judgment and ask myself, 'I wonder why they think that? I wonder what they can see that I can't see. Let me ask more questions about that.' And I wonder why I think I'm right." ~ *Kim Adele-Randall, CEO, Authentic Achievements*

I have one other phrase that goes with the technique to listen longer: **"If you're right now, you'll be right later."** If

Leadership Development

you realize this, you'll be able to wait to make your point in the discussion.

The Power of Respect

Respect is another essential ingredient in the success of a leader. Family members should respect each other's roles and contributions to the business, regardless of their position or title. This means that family members should not take advantage of their relationships with each other and should treat each other with the same level of professionalism and respect that they would show to a non-family member.

When family members respect each other, they can work together more effectively and avoid the kinds of conflicts that can tear family businesses apart. Respect also helps to build trust, which is essential in any business but even more critical in family businesses where personal relationships are so intertwined.

Respect builds trust, trust builds relationships, and relationships are the key to Leadership.

Being Clear About Results

Finally, family business leaders must be clear about the results they want to achieve. They should have a clear vision for the future of the business and communicate that vision to everyone involved. This means setting specific goals, creating a plan to achieve those goals, and holding everyone accountable for their contributions to the plan.

Family business leaders should also be willing to adapt their plans as circumstances change. This means being flexible and willing to make changes, when necessary, even if it means changing course or abandoning a previously established plan.

In conclusion, leadership development in family-owned, family-run businesses requires an approach that builds relationships both with family members, and in the event that they are non-family members, with the business leadership. By managing emotions, communicating effectively, showing respect, and being clear about the results they want to achieve, family business leaders can create a culture of success that will endure for generations to come.

Leadership Development

Leadership Development Thought Starters

Download the 8½ x 11 printable forms from:
ExpertsInHow.com/thought-starters

Does your business have a leadership development process?
Y ☐ N ☐

Does your family have a leadership development process?
Y ☐ N ☐

Example of a prospectus for leadership positions for family roles outside of technical management of the business:

Family Member Business Leadership Profile

Ideally, Family Member business leaders would have similar experiences and expertise as outside non-family leaders, but this is often not the case, especially as families grow. However, Family leaders have a distinct and critical role in the leadership and future of the company. For this reason, the criteria for Family member leadership that may not start with the technical skills typically found in non-family leaders. The important criteria for family member leaders are different than those of non-family leaders, though there can be considerable overlap.

The following are the criteria for Family Member Leadership:

1. Excellent problem-solving capabilities.
2. Ability to effect change.
3. Ability to communicate constructively with different groups (employees, other directors (if any), family, etc.), sometimes about difficult subjects.
4. Belief in the Values of the Family and the company.
5. Ability to communicate those Values meaningfully and constructively to the Board (if any),

management, and entire company, and ensure they are followed by the company.
6. Have the trust of the family.
7. Ability to communicate well with the family, both formally and informally.
8. Great listening skills to understand the current and future needs of the family.
9. Ability to articulate family needs to the board.
10. Are not beholden to a particular branch or branches of the family but feel loyalty to all.
11. Possess the confidence of the family.
12. Ability to win the confidence of other directors, including outside directors (if any), and management.
13. Ability to read and understand financial statements.
14. Respect for the board and governance processes.
15. Have sufficient self-confidence to ask questions and offer comments in governance related meetings, but the sense not to waste others' time in meetings.
16. Functional knowledge of areas such as strategy, strong business exposure, human resources, finance, marketing, and retailing are a plus.
17. Candidate has demonstrated a real interest in the business - primarily through participation in a variety of educational and engagement opportunities.
18. Candidate has a real commitment to future learning and development through personal investment of time in education sessions and mentorship opportunities to gain knowledge of the Company, the industry, board governance, financial statements, and risk management, etc. Willingness and eagerness to learn and develop.

Leadership Development

Typically, the criteria for candidates for non-family leadership roles will have technical skills needed to run the business based on the industry, markets, and company life cycle. Example of a prospectus for leadership positions requiring technical skills based on the needs of the business.

Non-Family Leadership Profile

Ideal candidates serve currently or have recently retired as CEO, President, COO, CFO, of a business with a minimum of $XXX million in revenue. It is expected that candidates are good communicators with strong character and integrity. They will have demonstrated in their careers strategic thinking, problem solving and the ability to effect change. They will also have board experience.

The Company values the following specific experience and expertise:

1. CEO level experience in businesses in excess of $XXX million revenues.
2. Senior leadership experience in the XYZ Industry, either on the market side or the supply side.
3. Successful track record of achieving strategic growth.
4. Mergers and Acquisition experience including integration.
5. Experience with digital transformation.
6. Relevant experience with succession planning.
7. Expertise in financial management, audit, and corporate control.
8. Family business experience, preferably including multi-generational transitions.
9. Manufacturing and supply logistics.
10. Experience with significant change management.

Chapter 8

SUCCESSION PLANNING

> "I will not be right back after this message."
>
> ~ *Merv Griffin's headstone*

What would happen to your business if you died tomorrow? Or if that's too harsh a question, let me ease into the conversation. What would happen to your business if you were laid up, unconscious, and unable to communicate with your team for three weeks? A month? Six months?

According to disability insurance statistics, every year 5.6% of working Americans will experience a short-term disability (usually six months or less).

A Gallop poll shows that nearly 40% of those with household incomes of $100,000 or more say they do *not* have a will.

Do you really want your state government to be put in charge of running your business after you die, while your family argues about succession?

As I said in the Introduction, succession planning has been the source of many of the great dramas throughout history. **It will always be a sensitive, challenging issue.**

While many businesses focus on short-term goals and day-to-day operations, it's essential to have a long-term plan to ensure that the business continues to thrive even after the current owners or leaders retire or pass away.

Succession planning is a process, not just a document. It involves identifying and preparing the next generation of leaders within the family to take over the business in some form as executives, board members, or owners. This includes identifying potential successors, providing them with the training and resources they need, and creating a plan for the transition. While generational engagement can inform succession planning, creating an actual succession plan and planning process is different from generational engagement. It's a question of knowing who's ready to step into your shoes, and whether you've prepared them the best way possible.

Family succession planning involves identifying the skills important to directing the business now, and in the future, and assessing if family members' experience fills those needed skill sets. Once any gaps are identified, generational engagement plays a role in preparing them for service and filling those gaps.

> "The best way to approach a transition or plan a succession is not to think about what's needed today, but about what will be needed in ten years. For obvious reasons, that's difficult to gauge, but you want the next crop of leaders to have even more talents and skills than the current team." ~ *Meghan Juday, Chair of the Board, IDEAL Industries*

Without a plan in place, this transition can be fraught with conflict and confusion, and it can put the future of the business in jeopardy.

By creating a succession plan, family-owned businesses can help to ensure that the transition is smooth and seamless. This not only protects the future of the business but also helps prevent family conflicts and misunderstandings.

One of the first steps in creating a succession plan is to identify what the business needs for leadership going forward. A concurrent step is to identify potential successors within the family. This involves taking a hard look at each family member's strengths, weaknesses, and interests, and identifying those who have the potential to lead the business. Creating a "gap analysis" of the skills needed by the business, and the skills of family candidates, is an important next step.

Once potential successors have been identified, along with any skill gaps, it's essential to provide them with the development plans and resources they need to succeed. This could mean offering mentorship or coaching programs, providing access to educational resources, or giving them opportunities to take on leadership roles within the company.

It's also important to create a plan for the transition of leadership. This could involve gradually transferring ownership and control of the business to the next generation, or it could involve a more abrupt transition. The key is to ensure that everyone is on the same page and that there's a clear plan in place for how the transition will take place.

Succession planning is that, combined with generational engagement and leadership development, should be an ongoing process. Constantly striving to understand the needs and expectations of each member of the family (including those not involved in the business) will mitigate potential conflicts and misunderstandings. When everyone is *clear* about their roles and responsibilities, *and* there is a plan in place for the transition of leadership, there's less room for confusion or miscommunication. This can mitigate or prevent family members from feeling left out or excluded from the decision-making process.

Another benefit of succession planning is that it can help to ensure the long-term success of the business. By preparing the next generation of leaders, you can ensure that the business continues to thrive for many years to come. This not only protects the financial well-being of the family but also creates a legacy for future generations to build upon.

Of course, creating a succession plan is not without its challenges. **Family dynamics can be complicated, and it can be difficult to navigate the various personalities and relationships.** However, by taking a collaborative and open approach to succession planning, providing every member the opportunity to understand what the business needs and how they fit in, or their development plan options, family-owned businesses can help to ensure that everyone's opinions and concerns are heard and addressed.

In any selection process there can be frustration and even bad feelings about those who are selected among those who are not. **The family architecture should be designed to handle these very real, very human emotions.** For example, the family council should be clear about the process for identifying candidates for succession, and the selection process itself. If there are well-developed relationships within the family, then the family council would be able to anticipate issues among family members. As importantly, the family leadership should develop a family member development plan to provide specific opportunities to address and evaluate experience gaps versus the needs of the business. It's one thing to tell someone they were not selected for a role. It's much more engaging and motivating to inform them of the opportunities to develop into those roles.

In addition to creating a succession plan, **it's also important to regularly review and update the plan as needed.** This could involve revisiting the plan every few years, or it could involve updating the plan in response to major changes within the family, or the business. By keeping the plan up to date, you can ensure that everyone is prepared for any changes or challenges.

In a family-owned business, succession planning applies to multiple levels. It includes a succession of roles for the senior management, including the CEO; the roles of the family, including the family council; and the roles of a board of directors or advisors, if there is one.

Each of these positions plays a key role in decision making, generational engagement, leadership development, and ultimately the family's ability to create a desired legacy.

Succession planning requires a great deal of forethought, strategic thinking, and careful execution. Here are some of the key steps that should be taken to ensure a successful succession plan for family-owned businesses.

Start Early and Plan Strategically

Succession planning should not be rushed. It's essential to start early and have a strategic plan in place to ensure the success of the transition. It starts with generational engagement.

Succession Planning

Family gatherings allow the members to get to know one another, and their feelings about each other and the business. The meetings and discussions of the family council allow emerging leaders of the family to know about all the important aspects of the business and its governance. Planned family engagement activities provide family members with a hands-on way to accumulate experience in the business side of governance.

A good succession plan requires time, thought, and careful consideration of all the possibilities. While family engagement can start as early as childhood, it's only a step in the process of building knowledge and evaluating fit. Over time, that culminates in a change of leadership in the specific roles mentioned above. Ideally, family-owned businesses should review their plan for succession in specific roles at least five years before the planned transition. In addition, there should be an ongoing contingency plan for emergency transitions based on the best available information at the time.

The first step in creating a successful succession plan is to identify the key positions. These positions will include critical leadership roles of the family *and* the business. Once these positions have been identified, family-owned businesses should start thinking about who might be the best fit for these roles.

Identify potential successors!

Who's ready to lead? That largely depends on your leadership development process. Paul Gumbinner, a recruiter in marketing account management, had what he called, "The 10% Rule."

> "You start a business. As it grows, you need to hire more people, so you go looking for someone exactly like yourself. Of course, there's no such person, so you settle for someone who has 90% of your skills and talents. When that team has to hire, they go through the same process; and by the fourth level you're looking at people who are 40% less than ideal. One day the

company founder meets one of those people in the hall and asks himself, 'Who hired that doofus?'" ~ *Paul S. Gumbinner, President (Ret) The Gumbinner Company*

Identifying potential successors is one of the most critical steps in succession planning. For the business, it's essential to consider all potential candidates, including family members, current employees, and external hires. Family-owned businesses need to ensure that the best candidates are selected based on their skills, qualifications, and experience.

For the family roles (family council, board of directors, or advisors) other than leadership of the business, there is usually a desire to retain as much family continuity as possible.

We've helped family businesses create a calendar of planned transition roles, along with an evaluation of the skills ideally required for those roles. Concurrently, you should maintain a list of potential candidates and an ongoing evaluation of their skills. Update this list, and the skills evaluations, annually.

One common mistake that family-owned businesses make is *assuming* that family members are the best candidates for leadership. While family members may have a strong desire to take over the business, they may not have the skills or experience necessary to succeed. This requires a slightly different filter in the event of a family member who may not have gained the key technical business skills in their career at the time when a position opens up.

The best way to navigate the differences in family backgrounds, versus outside candidates, is to create a written prospectus that describes the business, the role, and the skill sets required for a successful candidate. This prospectus should be the same for *any* candidate, family or outside, for *any* position requiring specific technical skills. There's an example of the skill requirement section of a prospectus for these positions in the Leadership Development Thought Starters section at the end of this chapter. You will notice the emphasis on a list of technical skills which would be developed based on the needs of the business.

> "CEOs and business owners should think a little more proactively about putting people in the room, whether they provide immediate value or not. Putting younger people in the room gives them that apprenticeship, they get that learning and teaching that comes from observing." ~ *Torsten Pieper, Associate Professor, University of North Carolina, Charlotte*

The prospectus for a *family* leadership role could be slightly different as it emphasizes the family representation skills needed. There is an example of the skill requirement section of a prospectus for these positions in the Thought Starters at the end of this chapter. You'll notice the emphasis on understanding and buying into family values, as well as understanding the commitment to responsibility and willingness to put in the work to learn and grow as a family leader and contributor to the company.

Develop and train potential successors

Once potential internal successors have been identified, family-owned businesses need to develop and train them to be successful in their future leadership roles. This can involve a variety of activities, such as mentoring, job shadowing, and leadership development programs. Family-owned businesses should also provide opportunities for potential successors to gain experience in different parts of the business, such as finance, operations, and sales.

It's essential to develop a robust development program tailored to the specific needs of each potential successor.

Communication

Another important aspect of succession planning is communication. Family businesses often have complex family dynamics, and it can be difficult to have open and honest conversations about the future of the company. However, it's essential to involve all family members in the process and to ensure that everyone is on the same page. Every family member should know and understand the process of succession planning, including what skills and experience are required to be successful. This allows every family member to understand their circumstances relative to the opportunities and the path they will need to take to be considered.

In addition to communication within the family, it's also important to involve external advisors. This can include lawyers, accountants, and business consultants who can provide objective advice and help to guide the process.

Balance the needs of the business and the family

Not everyone in the family will agree with your choice. This can be particularly challenging when there are multiple family members involved in the business. Often there's more than one family member who believes they're ready and able to step into the role of CEO. Without a family constitution or agreement that outlines the roles and responsibilities of each family member, and how these decisions will be made, I can guarantee there will be problems. It's important that family members understand that the needs of the business come first, so that the business can be successful in meeting the needs of the family. This does not preclude the need for and benefit of a development plan for family members to gain the skills and experience they need to manage or advise the business.

> "Some family businesses have an owners' academy where they come together for three, four, or five days, several times throughout the year. They spend a lot of time having fun together, but they also go through a specific curriculum where they're taught how to read a balance sheet. How do you make sense of basic financial ratios? What is strategy? How do you go about defining strategy and competition? It makes everybody

smart. So even of you're an opera singer in Paris, an engineer in Brisbane, or a teacher in New York, everyone has the same level of basic understanding. That gives you an ownership group who knows what you're talking about as a manager." ~ *Torsten Pieper, Associate Professor, University of North Carolina, Charlotte*

Financial considerations

Family businesses often have significant assets tied up in the business, and it's important to ensure that these assets are protected and transferred to the next generation in a tax-efficient manner. This may involve setting up trusts, creating buy-sell agreements, or implementing other estate planning strategies. Once again, I can't give you a one-size-fits-all rule. Each family and its subsequent generations need to determine what will work best. Consult with an expert, your accountant or tax attorney, to develop the most efficient strategy and instruments for this purpose.

Emotional considerations

It's difficult to set aside emotions when making succession decisions. Keeping focus on the various technical and family skill sets we've described will allow for a process that can be articulated and is as objective as possible. An objective approach can help avoid bad decisions. Using a literary example, here's a short list of Bad Ideas, starting with Machiavelli's *The Prince*, and going back to Sun Tsu's, *The Art of War*. Fortunately, we have William Shakespeare to serve as our coach and mentor.

Bad Idea:	**Case Study:**
Poor estate planning	"King Lear"
Pick the wrong heir	"Richard III"
Appoint your 2nd spouse	"Hamlet"

Disinherit someone	"Richard II"
Ignore resentments	"Macbeth"
Ignore your legacy	"King John"
Ignore your advisors	"Julius Caesar"

In conclusion, succession planning is a critical component of building a lasting legacy. By identifying potential successors, providing them with the training and resources they need to succeed, and creating a plan for the transition of leadership, family-owned businesses can help to ensure that the business continues to thrive for many years to come with the appropriate family involvement.

The first step is the hardest. If your family does not have a succession plan, establishing one will be emotionally challenging. **Do not be afraid, and do not wait!** Too often, the founder decides on a succession plan, has their personal attorney incorporate it into their will, and surprise the rest of the family after they've died.

Creating a meaningful, lasting family business legacy means *everyone* at every level and in every generation needs to be part of the planning process to protect their future and create a legacy that will sustain and grow.

Succession Planning Thought Starters

Download the 8½ x 11 printable forms from:
ExpertsInHow.com/thought-starters

A succession planning process is not just about checking boxes of skill sets. It is a process about transitioning relationships, and as such is inherently emotional. In preparation, ask yourself and your family these questions in order to surface some of the hard subjects that will need to be addressed:

1. Do you feel there is an adequate succession plan for the management of the business and the family?
2. What would you like to see as the transition of the business?
   - From a management perspective?
   - From a family perspective?
3. Are the incumbents ready to step aside?
4. Is family branch representation important?
5. Do gender or age preferences trump technical skills?
6. Has the selection process been clearly articulated and do members of the family understand the selection process?
7. Are there multiple opportunities for leadership available to family members and do family members understand what the opportunities are, the timing of those opportunities, and how they can access development plans to be ready.
8. Have you thought out development plans through generational engagement to provide opportunities for family members?

Chapter 9

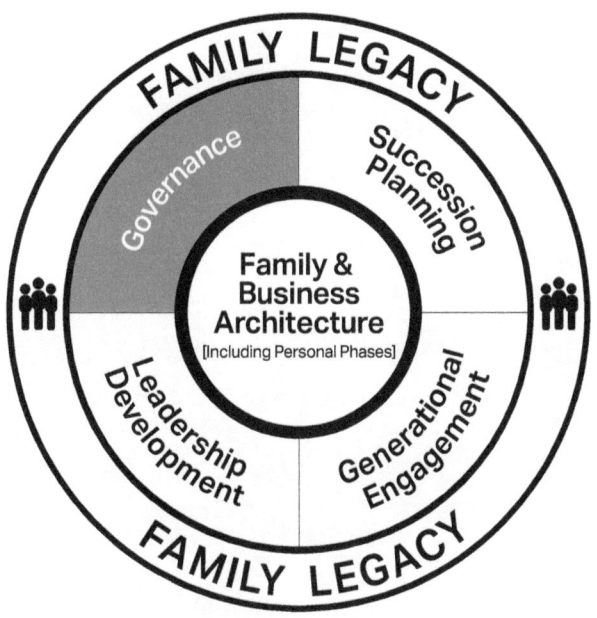

GOVERNANCE

> "I'm the decider, and I decide what's best."
> ~*President George W. Bush*

"Governance" is an emotionally loaded word to owners of a family business. For many founders and G2 owners, **their biggest fear is the mistaken belief that governance means an outsider is going to start telling them what to do.** Or, worse, someone else in the family will be looking over their shoulder second-guessing everything. There's also the fear that an outsider will come to understand the trade secrets of the business or have access to all the financials.

Those beliefs lead to a related issue, the inability to look objectively at key positions and ask whether an outsider with skills in one area would be a better hire than a family member for the same position.

Take a moment and ask yourself if you, or any member of your family ownership team, have ever held those beliefs.

- "I don't need someone else to tell me what to do."
- "This is our business, we'll run it our way."
- "Our company is too small to need a board of directors."
- "An outsider will just take our business secrets and go somewhere else."

"Governance" is an accepted legal and business term for the processes *you* put in place to make sure things get done properly within *your* given range. Most important for the long-term survival and growth of your business, those processes will get done even when you're not involved in every decision.

There's a freedom to governance that allows owners to concentrate on the actual business and the path of the business. Where are we now? Where are we going? How are we going to get there? What are our next steps? Who's going to do what? Who will be in charge in the event of [fill in the blank]? I hear people say, "Oh my God, governance is a terrible word. I don't like governance. I don't want anything to do with governance." Then I ask them, "How are you running your business?" and they say, "I do this, and I do that and nobody gets to write a check over X amount unless I sign for it, and all these Y decisions come through me."

I explain, "Well, that's governance." Did I make you feel better?

It's really no different from writing a new-employee manual. Governance helps family members, owners, investors, and employees understand the steps in running your business. Most important, whether you're involved as an owner, a manager, a board member, if you're part of the operational team then you control the process of governance. That's the watershed moment, when an owner understands that they're *already* doing governance; they just didn't know what to call it.

Governance provides the framework so owners and managers can navigate the different phases of their business. This includes approval levels, strategic discussions, and business reviews. It means understanding what you should do going forward, regardless of whether you do it yourself, or someone else does it for you.

Governance is about helping you manage the business, so things get done correctly. For example, when there's an approval level required to make an expenditure, it's usually a matrix. If it's this much, it goes to so-and-so; if it's that much, it goes to so-and-so. If it's above a certain amount, then it's always communicated to so-and-so for approval. Maybe you have a rule about pricing, the way car salespeople must "get my manger's approval" on the deal. Or the rule says you can't make a capital acquisition, buy a building, or buy a company, without my approval.

Entrepreneurial G1 owners need reassurance that "governance" won't mean someone else is telling them what to do and understanding that they will be part of shaping the initial governance and maintaining its form and application. The evolution of good governance is a continuous journey, even in a 100-year-old family business like Phillip's Flowers.

> "It's beneficial to have some directors on your board who aren't working in the family business. Dad and I started putting together a few outside directors, and much to our surprise, we were able to get a few guys who had a lot more experience and bigger businesses than we had, and they were willing to serve for really what was a pittance at the time, and that outside wisdom was helpful." ~ *Jim Phillip, CEO, Phillip's Flowers & Gifts*

Once people get past the idea that it's not somebody else telling them what to do, they start to see it as a process that makes sure things get done. Timetables. Values. Planning. R&D. Investing. Internal Controls. Whatever the owners see as necessary elements to growth and survival.

Good governance can add safeguards that wouldn't otherwise exist. One company we know established an internal whistleblower number for people in their company who have a complaint about an owner or partner. Confidentially, they can call that number and explain to HR directly, "Here's what my concern is," and then open it up for an investigation. Having the ability for people to appropriately challenge what's being done is good governance. Another is the ability for anyone to make productive suggestions for improvement. Making everyone feel that their ideas matter is a powerful way to reward and keep employees and associates.

A key element is how you treat the people who are going to be governed and how you explain the governance process. I invite you to read my book, *The Power of Respect in Business*. The first time we helped put in a governance requirement of an approval level matrix at a family-owned business, the senior management team said, "Wait a minute. You're going to tell me what I have to provide to the Board of Directors before I can decide on projects of a certain amount?" We explained the purpose; to make sure there were proper controls that are visible to the spending limits in the organization. It was not intended to keep anyone from doing their job. It was meant as a way for senior management to all be aware of what the company was going to spend, and what they were going to spend it on.

> "When a business starts at the founder's level, it's dominated by one person's vision, one person's decisions. It's very autocratic. I'm sure my grandfather was that way. When you get into the second generation, and maybe a son or a daughter or siblings get involved, you get multiple opinions—multiple people whose name is on the door, there must be a lot more deference to each other. Otherwise, you end up killing each other over minor things." ~ *Jim Phillip, CEO, Phillip's Flowers & Gifts*

> "[Without a set of rules], typically, I saw consistent elements that were broken across all the businesses, resulting in harm to their financials with negative cash flows, and maybe break-evens or losing money. The causal element always came down to the team. They were very often dysfunctional. Sometimes they fought with each other. Sometimes there was a lack of capability and aptitude to do the jobs that they wanted to do. There was virtually no strategy, and there was complacency involved. Eventually you must lay out ground rules" ~ *Steve Kosmalski, Fortune 100 Consumer Products Turnaround Executive*

Those "ground rules" are governance.

Part of the process is to show families what's historically good governance, what other companies consider best practices, and what's keeping their CFO or CEO from doing their best job. As you go down the path of describing what each issue is, you need to continue with the "why." Once you do the

Governance

root analysis, then you have a chance of solving problems you might not have known existed. It's not a set of orders. Crafting a healthy set of governance rules should include everyone's thinking.

Most companies already have some kind of governance process in place. You can't really operate any business without rules, and often people don't even think about it. They go into work; they know they have to punch a timecard if they have an hourly job. They don't question that. It's common sense and they understand it. Where the challenges arise is when the family discovers they must abide by the *same* set of rules. I often get pushback from senior people who are reluctant to change old habits. Again, if you explain it, they will come on board.

"Why do we have to do time sheets?" a family member asks. You explain, "Because we need to accurately understand the labor cost of the business, and the distribution of that labor cost to different activities as we make decisions about pricing, as we make decisions about how to make money, so that we can all be gainfully employed." Regardless of what level you're at, you must assume that it's better to explain to somebody why you're doing that, help them understand and help them out. Let them air their concerns. For example, let them ask, "If I have to punch a timecard, then I can't do this or that or the other thing." Well, let's understand what that is and make sure that we are accommodating that, or eliminating that, quite frankly, as a barrier to doing the task at hand.

Understanding "Why?" can go a long way to managing any situation. A friend started his career in a large advertising firm and resented the weekly time sheet requirement. He thought the company was trying to make sure he was busy. It was years before someone explained that it wasn't about him; it was the only way the company could assess and manage their client's costs.

Governance is the primary way to get a business to where it's supposed to be. It's the primary way to get any business under control. That's true for any business. And many family-owned businesses already know how to do some of that. It's not a case of having to start from ground zero, or just because it's a family-owned business. The best place to start is to assume there's nothing in place. **The word may have a sting instead of a ring to it, but if you ask yourself what you're doing, you are always and already doing governance.** You are executing the controls necessary to make sure the business meets your objective. It's in your best interest. When a lack of discipline or sloppiness sets in, it can very quickly cause a business to fail. The challenge is threefold:

1. How to get started (process)
2. How to bring everyone on board (agreement)
3. How to move in the new direction (implementation)

Process

Assess what you're already doing. Ask yourself, "Is this working for us, or is this an old process that isn't relevant anymore." Make every department head—whether they're family members or not—bring their own assessment to the table. Have them put it all in writing. I ask clients, "Can someone else do your job if you were out sick for a month? How would that impact your business?" Make sure everyone understands it's for the good of the company and the family.

Agreement

If everyone is on board, you're okay. If someone disagrees with the decisions, the direction, and the dictates of your governance policies, hear them out. See if they have a suggestion for improvement. If they're not willing to accept any form of governance, they will always be an obstacle to continued success and growth. We've all heard the expression, "If you're not part of the solution, you're part of the problem." That's never truer than in a family-owned, family-run business. As Steve Kosmalski goes on to say:

> "You can go into a closed-door room with the senior team and work things out and, hopefully, come out with agreements. In most cases you do, or at least you have a better path forward. Then the rest of the organization is really not hurt at all. You must communicate up and down. Get the organization's input, treat everyone with respect, but tell them, 'Here's a plan, here's why it's there, here's where it worked before.' Ask for their input, and if there's any good ideas that come in, integrate them within the organization." ~ *Steve Kosmalski, Fortune 100 Consumer Products Turnaround Executive*

Implementation

You must do what works best for your company. It might be as simple as a written Company Manual that explains how everything will be done. It might involve—as it did for Starbucks in May 2018—closing the entire company for a one-day global retraining. Or it might be as complex as when the British finally aligned their calendars with the solar year. People went to bed on Wednesday, September 2, 1752, and woke up on Thursday, September 14.[2]

In any event, it's critical to have some form of governance in place for the family to maintain appropriate control through the various personal and generational phases described in Chapter 3. Without a proper system and understanding of governance, family members will hesitate to allow the business to evolve beyond their immediate control. The result of that scenario will be to prevent the realization of the potential legacy

---

[2] There are numerous books and anecdotes surrounding that event, including parliamentary debates, religious discussions, and reports of riots. The biggest concern for many people was their belief that the government had just shortened their lives by 12 days!

of the business or family. This is one of the main reasons that family businesses often sell by G3.

Governance and Family Values

Governance is also an effective way to bring both employee family members and non-employee family members in line with the standards of the company. Within any best-in-class governance structure, family values are a key element incorporated throughout the governance structure. When you're a member of G2, G3 or more, it's easy to forget you have to hold yourself to a higher standard than an employee who is *not* a family member or owner. It's tempting to pull out a company credit card for personal expenses or operate as if the rules do not apply to you. That attitude is demoralizing, destructive, and deadly to any company. And if your business is publicly traded or operates under the rules of the SEC, FCC, FDA or any other legal umbrella, those behaviors and attitudes can even lead to jail time.

It's important to understand that governance structures exist, not just for Business Governance, but for Family Governance as well, which I talked about in Chapter 4 on Family and Business Architecture.

If you already have a governance structure in place, you know how challenging it is to keep it up to date, keep it relevant and keep everyone informed. Ask anyone who has a governance process what their business would look like without one and they will all tell you the same thing. They would be out of business. Jamie Shyer of Zyloware Eyewear summed it up perfectly when his company made a critical pivot. "We went from where we could have been out of business to becoming a first, second, or third tier supplier to the largest retail chains in the world."

Governance

Governance Thought Starters

Download the 8½ x 11 printable forms from: ExpertsInHow.com/thought-starters

There are whole libraries and entire college majors devoted to the subject of corporate governance. It can be overwhelming; especially since not all the information is relevant to your particular family's needs. But **start with the basics.** Ask (and answer) these few questions and you will quickly understand where your business and your family might be vulnerable.

Look at all the policies and procedures you expect your family and company to follow.

- Are there areas that you consider to be a risk to the cash management or return on investment?
- Do they include the policies you expect will protect your cash and return goals? Do some areas not have the appropriate rules?
- Would you benefit from an expert reviewing your situation for any gaps that can cause risk?
- Ask each team, "If [Head of Department] was out sick for six months, would the team know what needs to be done—and how?

List all the areas of Governance rules you currently have in place that may or may not be written down anywhere:

- Expenditures
- Investments
- Purchasing
- Pricing
- Hiring
- Buying or selling assets
- Cash receipts

- Inventory

Who is responsible for each of those areas?

_____
_____
_____
_____
_____
_____
_____

Is there a clear understanding of how the desires of the family are made known to the operating Management?
- Regarding appetite for debt?
- Mergers and Acquisition objectives?
- Dividend policy?
- Family employment policy?
- Bonus and other compensation issues?
- Elements of ESG?
- Other key issues?

_____
_____
_____
_____
_____

Chapter 10

RISK MANAGEMENT

> "Your greatest successes will often come from how you turn an obstacle into an opportunity."
>
> ~ *Lisa Cochrane, VP, Marketing, Allstate Insurance (Ret.)*

Lisa Cochrane once told the story of how the Allstate "Mayhem" campaign came to be. Dennis Haysbert was starring in their "Good Hands" campaign. One morning she was driving to the office thinking about how well everything was going. As we remember it, she said, **when she gets complacent, that's when she gets concerned.**

For much of human history, there was no concept of "managing risk." In the mid-1500s, two French mathematicians, Blaise Pascal, and Pierre de Fermat, unlocked the mathematics of probability.[3] Prior to that, people believed that everything that happened to them was "fate" or "in the hands of the gods."

Since the earliest days of risk management, that balance between numbers and fate has always defined the tension between managers and entrepreneurs.

> "[It's] the persistent tension between those who assert that the best decisions are based on quantification and numbers, determined by the patterns of the past, and those who base their decisions on more subjective degrees of belief about the uncertain future. **This is a controversy that has never been resolved.**" ~ *Peter L. Bernstein, author, Against the Gods: The Remarkable Story of Risk*

Sometimes that tension is in our own way of thinking, as William Goodspeed said:

---

[3] Sometimes human progress comes from less-than-noble reasons. They were asked to evaluate gambling probabilities by a wealthy compulsive gambler who was looking for a competitive edge against the house.

"I went to law school after I graduated from college, then worked at McKinsey & Co., which had an extremely analytical way of thinking. Then I had to unlearn through those years the power of inspiring leadership and relationships... You can do the analysis like crazy, but you've got to have an emotional connection to people." ~ *William Goodspeed, Board Chair & Independent Director*

We may all hate risk, but without it, there's no possibility of growth or change. As much as you hoped I was going to remove all risk from your organization, here's the reality. To create value, every business organization must plan for and produce a financial return to compensate the shareholders or owners for the risk of their investment in the business. It's a process that helps the key people in your organization discover:

- What the business should become.
- The risk of different strategic alternatives.
- How to build corporate value through continuous renewal.

As a process, this helps management create an understanding of the environment in which the organization operates, which includes identifying the internal and external risks you face.

Note, the term is "managing" risk, is not the same as "controlling" it. I was leading a seminar for business owners talking about risk management, and one attendee told the story about a camp for children, and the board of advisors brought in their insurance agent and their legal counsel who said, "You need to eliminate risk." One of the members sitting there said, "Let me get this straight. We're going to have a camp where no one can shoot a bow and arrow. No one can get into the water. No one can light a campfire." And everyone immediately understood the absurdity of eliminating all risk.

Risk Management

Some risks we face are inherent in what we do (farmers need rain, consumers are fickle) and some we take on deliberately (deciding what crops to plant or what style of clothing to make). **Enterprise Risk Management (ERM) is the approach we take to identify, analyze, respond to, and monitor risks and opportunities around our choices and decisions.** Let's start with some definitions and objectives:

- Enterprise Risk Management (ERM) is the management of risks that have to be taken to achieve strategic objectives.
- ERM is the responsibility of your operating leadership team under direction of the Board of Directors or ownership committee.

Objectives of ERM:

- Ensure a consistent risk management approach.
- Support a strong risk culture throughout the organization.
- Promote risk awareness and sound operational and strategic decision-making.
- Ensure we only take risks of a type and level that the organization has agreed are acceptable—our organization's risk appetite.

By identifying and proactively addressing risks and opportunities, we protect and create value for our stakeholders. And by identifying and separating the different types of risk, we make the entire process more manageable.

While there are dozens of different risks, I find there are four overarching categories that help my clients organize their company's thinking:

Strategic Risk

The risk that we will fail to identify strategic opportunities or threats that are material to the company, or to define appropriate strategic responses, thereby leaving such opportunities or threats unaddressed. These risks include fundamental questions about our operating model, go to market approaches, and broader industry trends (e.g., two-step distribution, digital, retail, etc.).

Operational Risk

The risk of loss resulting from inadequate or failed internal processes, people, and systems, or from external events, including legal risk, supply chain risk, distribution risk. Examples include weaknesses in operational processes, people and systems associated with operational controls, including information and cybersecurity. People risks include potential loss or reputational damage due to not having the right people with the right skills doing the right thing, and failure to implement appropriate succession planning.

Financial Risk

The risk of financial loss because of business activities, including failure of internal controls.

Compliance Risk

The risk that we fail to observe the letter and spirit of laws, codes, rules, regulations, and standards of good market practice such as environmental and regulatory, safety, and trade and tariffs.

Each of those categories has additional elements that need to be addressed separately.

Different companies might choose to organize the risks in different ways, but what matters is that **all foreseeable risks are evaluated.**

An associate was a volunteer EMT in his younger days. As part of his training, he had to take an EMT safe driving course. The instructor started the course by saying, "You're driving

Risk Management

down the road on a bright, sunny morning, wide awake, doing the speed limit. Suddenly a meteorite comes hurtling down from space and smashes into the hood of your car." He paused. "That's an accident. Everything else is driver error."

Will you face unexpected problems? Always. And you will also face unexpected opportunities. By having a Risk Management process and team in place, your family and your company will be able to logically evaluate any situation.

Of course, the process is continuous. Every quarter, the management team and executive board should review the risk report and make appropriate situational changes and recommendations.

The process diagram looks like this:

For family-owned, family-run businesses, there's the added risk of "family," and the added risk factor of "reputational risk." Most publicly owned businesses don't think about their reputational risk until they encounter it head on. Think about all the incidents you've seen in the news about a company having to back-pedal something they did or said. Almost all the time, those are not family-owned, family-run businesses.

We are all much too aware of our legacy and how important our reputation is.

"Risk" doesn't mean you've done something wrong or will do something wrong. It's a recognition that all businesses face uncertainties that must be considered. The key is to recognize which risks matter.

Let us say you owned a hamburger spot in Charlotte, North Carolina, and a war breaks out in Ukraine. Spending business time on the war does not help you much because it's not related. On the other hand, if you have a fleet of trucks running on diesel fuel and a war breaks out in a country which is a conduit for energy—a pipeline, a refining plant, a port—that *does* affect you. And the fact that you're aware that supply chain is a risk for you, means you must pay attention to news and other things that might be indications in advance of the domino that's going to affect you. How many companies have you heard about who got caught flat-footed when COVID-19 disrupted their supply chain? Did you try to buy a new car between 2020-2023? Suddenly, Tesla's decision not to outsource their software looked very, very smart.

Every company should have a planning session where participants break down the critical parts of their business and identify which variables might impact their processes and bottom line. It's a process. It's a journey. It is not a sprint to be able to understand what the risk environment is and how to manage it effectively.

That same thinking should go into your risk assessment for your family, especially if there are owners who are not part of the business. For example, what if you were thinking about buying a pulp mill, and Great Aunt Betty is a ferocious environmentalist? You risk a lawsuit from your own family, not just from an outside source.

That's the other aspect of Risk Management. It is a tool to reduce surprises. Surprises should be reserved for birthday

Risk Management 139

parties. The more you can objectively view your business and family landscape, the less likely you will be caught by surprise.

Risk Management Thought Starters

Download the 8½ x 11 printable forms from: wwwExpertsInHow.com/thought-starters

Here's a sample of the worksheets I have companies complete as they assess the risks in their organization.

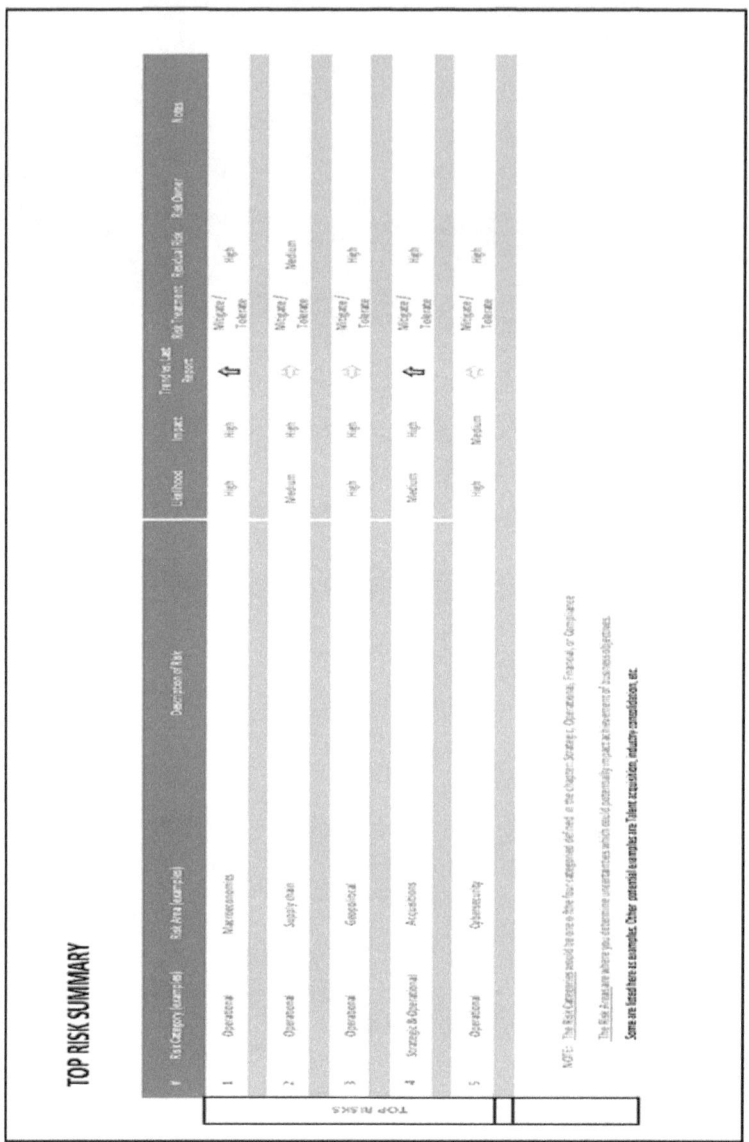

Risk Management

The key to risk management is measurement. A basic rule is, "You can't manage what you don't measure." Whether you download my templates or create your own, I believe there are key metrics that must be considered in every business. Let us take a look at the TOP RISK SUMMARY form column-by-column:

The first column is numeric for tracking purposes. In a call or meeting is easier for people to find "Number 5" than it is to search for its name.

The second column is **Risk Category.** By that I mean what area of the business does the risk impact? Is it a Strategic Risk? An Operational Risk? A Compliance Risk? Make sure your team agrees on the categories and terms so each manager fills out their section in a way everyone can understand.

Third column is **Risk Area.** Think of this as a more detailed description of each Risk Category. If you listed Operational Risk in the second column, Risk Category is where you get specific. Is the Operational Risk a Supply Chain concern? Regulatory? Different businesses will need to decide what is a Risk Category and what is a Risk Area. For example, if you are a Financial Services firm, you might need to make "Regulatory" a Category and then identify different areas such as "SEC Compliance," "State Regulations," and so on. The columns are broad enough to customize it for each of your needs.

The fourth column is a **Description of Risk.** Here you need to provide enough information so your Risk Management Team can understand the issue and grasp its significance.

Column Five is the **Likelihood** that the risk will occur. Again, your team needs to agree on a rating system that is clear to everyone. Generally, I recommend a rating system from 1 to 5.

Column Six is the assessment of the **Impact** any particular risk will have on your business. Like the previous column, your team needs to agree on a rating system which is clear and relevant.

Column Seven is the ongoing Trend vs Last Report. Is the risk getting higher, lower or still the same?

Column Eight is **Risk Treatment.** This is an assessment of the best course of action. Should the risk be mitigated? Can it be tolerated? Should the company compete or ignore the actions of a competitor?

Column Nine is **Residual Risk.** When a risk is addressed by your team, it often is never eliminated, just controlled. The question then becomes, "What next?" This is an explanation of your ongoing course of action.

Column Ten is **Risk Owner**. Who is responsible for addressing the risk and coming up with solutions.

In my experience, those ten columns can give any business of any size an "executive summary" or "planning protocol" for all situations.

Other forms that help define and clarify the situation are:

Chapter 11

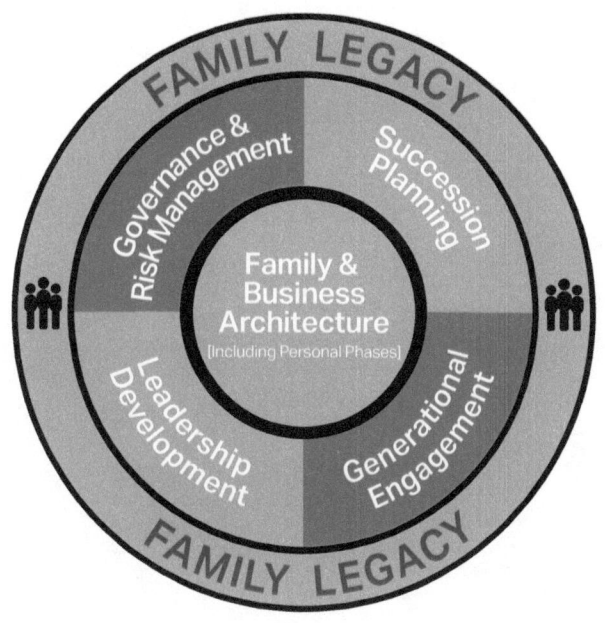

NEXT STEPS

Let's take a fresh look at the diagram in the Legacy Thought Starters section. Given all that you've now learned and thought about, let us offer you a different way of looking at this:

Are they up to speed on:	Legacy	Personal Phase	Family & Business Architecture	Generational Engagement	Leadership Development	Succession Planning	Governance	Risk Management
Who								
Family members with no business ownership (yet)								
Family members/owners								
Family members/employees								
Family employees								
Non-family/non-manager owners								
Non-family owner/employees								
Non-family employees								

Now you have your blueprint going forward.

    It's your family.

    It is your business.

    It is your knowledge.

    It is your responsibility.

    Get to work!

One last thought:

Do not let yourself get overwhelmed. While this book might feel intimidating, if you break the problem down into bite-sized pieces, you can create a family business legacy that will stand for years. And let me leave you with one thought from Walter Davis.

> "Owning your own business or having a family business gives you freedom. And some people don't really understand the freedom that you get. There's that freedom to succeed, the freedom to fall down and get back up. So failure is only when you stop trying. That's what owning your own business and the whole legacy piece gives you. Part of that is the freedom to be able to think differently and to expose the next generation to things that you think they should be exposed to. And they make up their own minds. Your job is just to expose them. And that, for me, in business is important." ~ *Walter Davis, Founding Member, Peachtree Providence Partners*

About the Author

Charlie Leichtweis is one of those rare individuals who can help you understand WHAT your organization needs to be doing and HOW to do it.

With more than 40 years' experience, he specializes in serving family businesses as a C-suite executive, consulting advisor, and as a board member.

He's the founder of Experts in How, LLC, a business consultancy focused on helping family-owned businesses with HOW to meet the challenges they face. He has identified the connection between the major elements related to creating and sustaining a successful legacy and HOW to manage those elements.

Charlie has global, strategic, operational, and financial leadership experience with a record of success in helping organizations achieve sustainable, profitable growth. Prior to Experts in HOW, Charlie shared his experiences as an advisor to clients as a Partner with Phoenix Strategic Advisors, and as Managing Director of Process Solutions, Inc.

He has held a number of C-suite roles including, CEO and President of The Testor Corporation, COO of North American Wholesale Group of Blyth Inc., CFO of Rand McNally Book Services, and CFO and Comptroller of Rust-Oleum Corp.

Charlie has taught graduate school and is the author of top selling books on business leadership and legacy. He's host of the podcast, "The Power of Respect," a popular keynote speaker, and he serves as a member of the Board of Directors for several companies.

Also by Charlie Leichtweis

The Power of Respect in Business - Enabling your teams to achieve sustainable profitable growth.

Important secrets to leadership excellence. Includes more than a dozen interviews with C- suite executives.

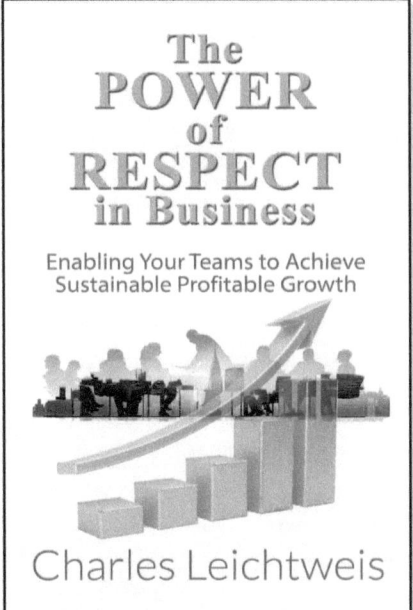

You will discover:

- R E S P E C T in action
- Use of the Emotional Scale to become a more effective leader and motivate others
- 8 secrets to achieving desired results faster.
- Practical examples of effective leadership
- How to create a culture of sustainable success

Available from Amazon.com

A Special Invitation

My years in business have shown me that consultants could always tell you WHAT should be done.... They simply could not tell you HOW. That's when I realized I could bring extra value to business consulting.

Thank you for reading *The Power of Legacy*. I hope it has helped you clarify your plans for success and succession. If you're still working on it, that's great. Just identifying your vulnerabilities will transform your business. I'd love to hear from you.

You can Email me Charlie@Expertsinhow.com and let me know what you're up to, or, Check out my website www.ExpertsInHow.com for many free resources to assist you on your journey.

Click on "SCHEDULE A FREE 30 MINUTE CONSULTATION" box in the upper left-hand corner. Make an appointment and I'll be glad to work with you.

Tune into my podcast, "The Power of Respect" for ongoing insights and inspiration. You can search all episodes of my podcast by title or guest on my website by pasting the following link in your browser and scrolling down.

https://expertsinhow.com/family-business-podcast/

"The Power of Respect" podcast can also be found on Spotify, Apple, or Google."

– Charlie Leichtweis

www.ingramcontent.com/pod-product-compliance
Lightning Source LLC
Chambersburg PA
CBHW020656060526
44119CB00090B/402/J